6x 3/05

MAR 2 2 2005

TEENS

Family & Issues

HAL MARCOVITZ

THE GALLUP YOUTH SURVEY:
MAJOR ISSUES AND TRENDS

Teens and Alcohol

Teens and Family Issues

Teens and Race

Teens, Religion, and Values

Teens and Sex

Teens and Suicide

TEENS
Family & Issues

HAL MARCOVITZ

Produced by OTTN Publishing, Stockton, New Jersey

Mason Crest Publishers
370 Reed Road
Broomall, PA 19008
www.masoncrest.com

3 5 7 9 8 6 4 2

Library of Congress Cataloging-in-Publication Data

Marcovitz, Hal.
  Teens and family issues / Hal Marcovitz.
      p. cm. - (The Gallup youth survey, major issues and trends)
Summary: Uses data from the Gallup Youth Survey and other sources to examine
the issue of teen family relationships in today's world.
Includes bibliographical references and index.
  ISBN 1-59084-725-3
1. Teenagers-United States-Family relationships-Juvenile literature. 2. Parent
and teenager-United States-Juvenile literature.
[1. Family. 2. Parent and teenager.] I. Title. II. Series.
  HQ796.M2788 2004
  306.874-dc22
                                        2003018514

Contents

Introduction

By George Gallup

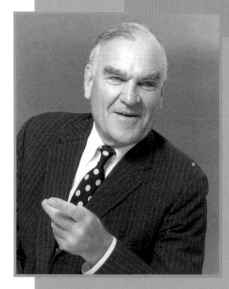

As the United States moves into the new century, there is a vital need for insight into what it means to be a young person in America. Today's teenagers—the so-called "Y Generation"—will be the leaders and shapers of the 21st century. The future direction of the United States is being determined now in their hearts and minds and actions. Yet how much do we as a society know about this important segment of the U.S. populace who have the potential to lift our nation to new levels of achievement and social health?

The nation's teen population will top 30 million by the year 2006, the highest number since 1975. Most of these teens will grow up to be responsible citizens and leaders. But some youths face very long odds against reaching adulthood physically safe, behaviorally sound, and economically self-supporting. The challenges presented to society by the less fortunate youth are enormous. To help meet these challenges it is essential to have an accurate picture of the present status of teenagers.

The Gallup Youth Survey—the oldest continuing survey of teenagers—exists to help society meet its responsibility to youth, as well as to inform and guide our leaders by probing the social and economic attitudes and behaviors of young people. With theories abounding about the views, lifestyles, and values of adolescents, the Gallup Youth Survey, through regular scientific measurements of teen themselves, serves as a sort of reality check.

We need to hear more clearly the voices of young people, and to help them better articulate their fears and their hopes. Our youth have much to share with their elders—is the older generation really listening? Is it carefully monitoring the hopes and fears of teenagers today? Failure to do so could result in severe social consequences.

Surveys reveal that the image of teens in the United States today is a negative one. Teens are frequently maligned, misunderstood, or simply ignored by their elders. Yet two decades of the Gallup Youth Survey have provided ample evidence of the very special qualities of the nation's youngsters. In fact, if our society is less racist, less sexist, less polluted, and more peace loving, we can in considerable measure thank our young people, who have been on the leading edge on these issues.

And the younger generation is not geared to greed: survey after survey has shown that teens have a keen interest in helping those people, especially in their own communities, who are less fortunate than themselves

Young people tell the Gallup Youth Survey that they are enthusiastic about helping others, and are willing to work for world peace and a healthy world. They feel positive about their schools and even more positive about their teachers. A large majority of American teenagers report that they are happy and excited about the future, feel very close to their families, are likely to marry, want to have children, are satisfied with their personal lives, and desire to reach the top of their chosen careers.

But young adults face many threats, so parents, guardians, and concerned adults must commit themselves to do everything possible to help tomorrow's parents, citizens, and leaders avoid or overcome risky behaviors so that they can move into the future with greater hope and understanding.

The Gallup Organization and the Gallup Youth Survey are enthusiastic about this partnership with Mason Crest Publishers. Through carefully and clearly written books on a variety of vital topics dealing with teens, Gallup Youth Survey statistics are presented in a way that gives new depth and meaning to the data. The focus of these books is a practical one—to provide readers with the statistics and solid information that they need to understand and to deal with each important topic.

* * *

Teens today face problems and pressures that their counterparts in earlier decades did not experience. Unfortunately, for many young people, the support system of a strong family has been torn apart today by divorce and other factors.

In this clearly written book, the author examines elements that undermine family relationships, but he points also to specific and concrete steps that can be taken to bring teens and parents closer together. With supporting data from surveys and other sources, the book examines the impact on teens of the entertainment industry, health matters, the effects of fatherlessness and divorce, the role of grandparents, and many other topics. A particularly interesting section of the book deals with home schooling, a relatively new social phenomenon touching many teens.

A constant theme in this book is that teens today need family support and guidance more than ever. They want help in making the right choices and—contrary to a common assumption—teens want more, not less, parental involvement. The real heroes in the lives of teenagers are their mothers and their fathers.

Chapter One

The Osbournes are perhaps one of the most famous families in the United States today, thanks to an MTV television series about their home life. Despite being the children of an international rock-and-roll star, Jack and Kelly Osbourne must deal with many of the same problems other teenagers face.

How Do Teenagers and Parents Get Along?

Each week's episode started with Wally and his younger brother, Theodore, ambling down a sun-kissed street in the mythical town of Mayfield. Carefree, the two boys headed home after a day at school. There they would be greeted by a loving mother eager to serve up a plate of cookies and glasses of milk. After homework Theodore, known as "the Beaver," would probably find a friend for a game of catch. Wally would likely start calling girls in search of a date to the school dance.

Americans loved *Leave It to Beaver*. For six years, millions of fans tuned in to watch the exploits of the Cleaver family. By the time the series went off the air in 1963, fans watched the Beaver grow into a teenager and Wally mature into a young adult.

There were a few bumps along the way, despite how perfect the family situation seemed. Wally or the Beaver would find a way to get into some sort of mischief, but both boys were good-hearted, and

A promotional photo of the cast of the television series *Leave It to Beaver*. The fictional Cleaver family does have one thing in common with the Osbournes—in both families, children and parents worked at communicating with each other.

would strive to come up with a solution to their problem. Invariably, they would get themselves in more hot water. At the end of each week's show, the boys' stern but sensible father Ward would hear all sides and come up with a solution that seemed to satisfy everyone while, of course, teaching the boys a valuable lesson.

The Cleaver home is hardly typical of most American households in the 21st century. Many teenagers have far greater problems and pressures facing them than those depicted on *Leave It to Beaver*. Any young person who tunes in to the TV reality show *The Osbournes* would observe vast differences between the problems faced by Wally and the Beaver and those faced by Kelly and Jack Osbourne, the teenage offspring of quirky heavy metal star Ozzy Osbourne. The advice Ozzy gives Kelly and Jack is certainly a lot different than what Ward gave. When, for example, the issue of drugs and alcohol use surfaces in the Osbourne house, Ozzy counsels his kids to steer clear of getting high or drunk. "It ain't gonna lead to nowhere but bad places," explains Ozzy, a recovering drug addict. "Look at me."

Despite differences in lifestyles, haircuts, and difficult issues, there is one common thread that ties the Cleaver family of 1963 with the Osbournes of 2003: Wally and Beaver Cleaver communicated and got along well with their parents, just as Jack and Kelly Osbourne communicate and get along well with their parents.

Spending Time Together

New York Senator and former first lady Hillary Rodham Clinton takes her role as a parent seriously and has stressed the importance of good parenting. "Teenagers need the guidance and support of their parents more than ever," she said. Her daughter, Chelsea, was nearly 13 when President Bill Clinton took office, and she spent the rest of her teen years in the White House during his two terms. When Hillary Clinton convened the White House Conference on Teenagers in May 2000, she asserted that a healthy relationship between teens and parents is well in reach:

> It is still difficult for many of us to remember that teenagers want our attention. After all, this is the time when the real or the imaginary "keep out" signs start appearing on closed bedroom doors, when many of our children would rather spend two hours talking to a friend on the phone than 10 minutes talking to their mother or father in person. But what we are learning is that for all their declarations of independence, America's teenagers still want and need the everyday love, involvement and discipline of their parents.

The Gallup Organization, a national polling firm, has long been interested in the attitudes and beliefs of young people, particularly when it comes to their relationships with their parents. As part of an ongoing project known as the Gallup Youth Survey, the organization has asked teenagers how well they get along with their parents, among other questions. The first year that the Gallup Youth Survey asked teenagers this question was 1977, when 97 percent of the respondents said they get along with their parents. Of that total, 56 percent stated that they get along "very

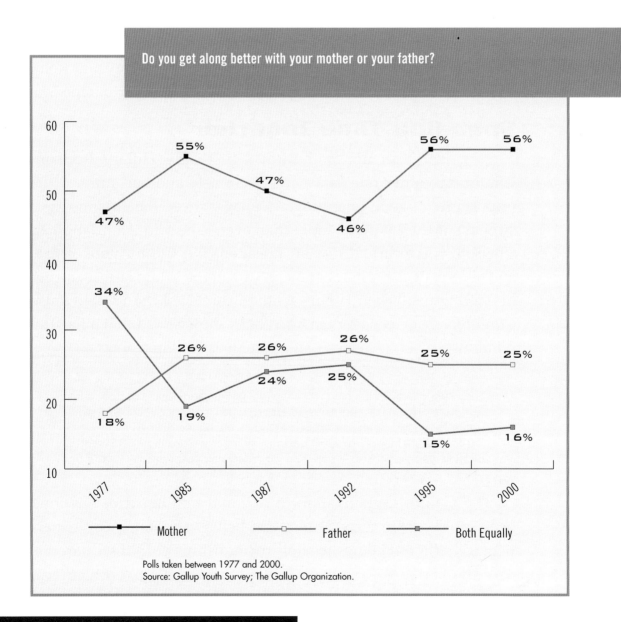

Do you get along better with your mother or your father?

Polls taken between 1977 and 2000.
Source: Gallup Youth Survey; The Gallup Organization.

well" with their parents and 41 percent stated they get along "fairly well" with them.

Subsequent findings have been consistent over the years. In 2000, a total of 501 young people between the ages of 13 and 17 participated in the same poll. Again, 97 percent of respondents to the Gallup Youth Survey said they get along with their parents. Of that number, 54 percent said they get along "very well" while 43 percent said they get along "reasonably well."

The 2000 poll also reported that teenagers not only get along with their parents, they also like doing things with them and being in their company. This response runs against the notion shared by many people—including some parents—that teens just want to be left alone. Other statistics indicate that people are mis-informed about teens and parents: the Gallup Youth Survey found that 68 percent of the respondents said an adult is usually home when they get home from school each day, and 55 percent said they pursue leisure activities with their parents on weekends. Sixty-eight percent said they wish they could spend more time with their fathers, and 64 percent said they'd like to spend more time with their mothers; 71 percent said their family usually eats at least one meal together, while 69 percent said they really enjoy mealtime.

Many people regard mealtime as a major influence in the lives of young people. Even the former president and first lady of the United States found time in their busy schedules to have dinner with their daughter. The Clintons made a commitment to Chelsea that although she could not have a normal adolescence, they would at least try to be normal parents. Her father held what is arguably the hardest job in the world, but President Clinton still found time to help his daughter with her homework.

Former president and first lady Bill and Hillary Clinton hold their daughter Chelsea's hand after her graduation from Stanford University in June 2001. Although while Chelsea was growing up her parents were among the busiest people in the world, they always made time for her.

"When Chelsea had to stay up all night adding footnotes to a research paper in high school, she appreciated our willingness to stay up with her, even though we were useless when her computer became temperamental," recalled Hillary Clinton. "When she became a vegetarian, the three of us bought vegetarian cookbooks. When she was getting ready for college, we went shopping for extra-long sheets, shower caddies and all those other necessities of dorm life."

The Clintons also made the effort to have at least one meal a day with their daughter. Sitting around the dinner table in the family's living quarters in the White House, the Clintons would ask their daughter the same questions most Americans ask their teenagers: How was school? How was the game? How did you do on that math test? How are your friends?

"One of the biggest casualties of modern life is family time—that time when parents and children can check out of their busy schedules and check in with each other," said Hillary Clinton. "Before our daughter left for college, my husband and I made it a priority to share at least one meal with her every day. It wasn't always easy, but we made the effort, and that half-hour in the small kitchen of our private quarters was my favorite part of the day."

To prepare for the White House Conference on Teenagers, the Council of Economic Advisers drafted a report on how well parents communicate with their teens. The report found that meal-time is a key time of day for parents to share ideas with their sons and daughters, and that teenagers who eat at least one meal a day with their parents are less likely to try risky behavior and more likely to do well in school and other activities.

The report also revealed other numbers about teens and the regular family meal:

> Less than 30 percent of 15- and 16-year-old teens who eat dinner with their parents have been involved in serious fights at school, a rate 10 percent lower than that of young people who don't eat dinner with their parents.

> Teenagers who share meals regularly with their parents generally have higher grade-point averages, are more likely to go to college, and are less likely to be suspended in school than teens who don't share meals with parents.

The following results were found about teens who don't eat dinner with their parents:

Thirty-four percent smoke, a rate that is 9 percent higher than teens who do eat dinner with their parents.

More than 50 percent reported that they have had sex by the age of 15; in contrast, 32 percent of teens who eat with their parents said they have had sex.

This teenage group is also three times more likely than other teenagers to entertain thoughts of suicide, and the suicide attempt rate for the 15- and 16-year-olds of the group is twice as high.

Bridging the Communication Lines

Whether parents and teenagers talk around the dinner table or other times during the day, there is no question that many of them do talk things out, although some mental health professionals wonder who is doing most of the talking. University of Maryland researcher Andrew Wolvin says that when it comes to communicating with their adolescent children, parents would do well to talk less and listen more. "We are so invested in our kids' lives that it's difficult to just be a sounding board when they want to talk," said Wolvin. "Everybody in America wants to run around dispensing advice. Instead, let your teenager articulate the problem and think of a solution."

For a story printed in 1999, *Ladies Home Journal* magazine wanted to find out how well parents and their teenagers communicated, and whether they truly did understand the points of conflict between them. The magazine posed questions to several sets of parents and their teenage children. Certainly there were disagreements, but on many topics the parents and teens were surprised to find themselves on the same page. For example, when a reporter asked Minneapolis, Minnesota, residents Nancy Robinson and her eighth-grade daughter Grace to name the hardest part of being a teen, Nancy said, "Adults often don't trust teens to make decisions about what's best for them." Grace agreed: "My parents treat me like I'm old enough to handle adult responsibilities—doing my own laundry, for instance—but they won't let me stay out later than 11 P.M."

When Houston, Texas, residents Lisa Studtmann and her 11th-grade son Jon were asked to define the household rule that Jon finds most objectionable, they both named the family curfew. Lisa told the interviewer that Jon's curfew is midnight on weekends and subject to his parents' discretion on school nights. "In the summer, they always want me home early on weeknights," Jon

Although it is important for parents to give advice and direction to their children, they should also be able to simply listen if their children wish to discuss things that are bothering them.

complained. "My dad has to get up early in the morning and my parents claim they can't go to sleep until I get home. I don't understand that."

And when the magazine asked Ventura, California, residents Dave Le Sueur and his 11th-grade son Daniel Weireter when the proper time would be to start having sex, Dave thought that during his son's college years would be the most appropriate time. "A lot of my dad's responses make sense," said Daniel. "He's a parent, so of course he hopes I won't have sex until I'm in college."

These few positive examples do not necessarily represent how all teenagers and their parents discuss pressing issues over the dinner table or at other times. In fact, many teenagers and their parents simply aren't interested in maintaining lines of communication. "You are who you hang around with," California teenager Venesa

UNLIKELY HEROES

The Gallup Youth Survey has found that not only do teenagers get along with their parents, they often look up to them. In 2003 the survey asked 1,200 young people between the ages of 13 and 17 to name the man and woman they admire most. President George W. Bush, Secretary of State Colin Powell, rap star Eminem, former basketball star Michael Jordan, singers Britney Spears and Avril Lavigne, entertainer Jennifer Lopez, and U.S. Senator Hillary Rodham Clinton all made the list. But the people teens admire most turned out to be their parents. Overall, mothers received 11 percent of the votes, while fathers scored 7 percent of the responses.

In 2002, the Gallup Organization released results of a similar survey in which it asked teenagers, "Do you have any heroes or heroines in the world today—men or women whom you personally greatly admire for their achievements and for their strong moral character?" Out of 500 respondents, 23 percent selected family members. Family members received more responses than sports figures (who

Vathanasombat told a news reporter in 2000. "Before, parents made you who you are. Now, teens are pretty much defined by their friends. I see my mom maybe an hour a day and not at all on weekends."

Also, because some families openly hold discussions does not necessarily mean that all problems simply go away. Today, many teenagers face problems that certainly would have stumped even Ward Cleaver back in 1963. Jack Osbourne did talk over his substance abuse with his father, who attempted to steer him clear of drugs and alcohol. Even after receiving that fatherly advice, however, Jack didn't listen. In the spring of 2003, the 17-year-old checked himself into a drug and alcohol rehabilitation facility.

Jack isn't the only teenager with problems. According to the Council of Economic Advisers report, as many as 15 percent of all teens are obese and many others have nutrition problems, such as

received 14 percent), musicians (8 percent), spiritual and human rights figures (6 percent), or actors and other entertainment personalities (3 percent).

Dr. Peter Gibbon, a research associate at the Harvard Graduate School of Education and author of the book *A Call to Heroism: Renewing America's Vision of Greatness*, says heroes are different from typical pop idols, movie stars, athletes, and other celebrities in that "heroes must do something spectacular that is a model for others."

Even in an age when teenagers are assaulted with the media's coverage of pop icons, the Gallup Youth Survey results indicate that for many teenagers, the real heroes doing spectacular things are still the people who help get them up in the morning, make their breakfast, and get them ready for the day ahead.

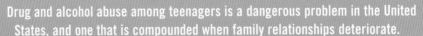

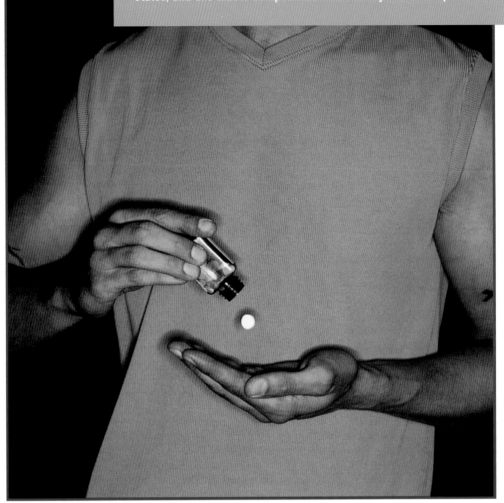

calcium deficiencies. Gun use is a problem among teens, with guns responsible for 85 percent of teen homicides and 63 percent of teen suicides. Although teen pregnancy rates are dropping, some 900,000 girls under the age of 18 still become pregnant every year. Cigarette use continues to be widespread among young people, with some 4 million teenagers a year regularly lighting up.

These are all risky behaviors. Nevertheless, experts believe teenagers' habits are likely to become less risky after they talk things over with their parents. The Council of Economic Advisers explains the importance of maintaining open lines of communication:

> [P]arental bonds help teens face today's difficult decisions and serious risks to their well-being. Though many harmful and destructive behaviors among teens are on the decline—including youth violence, teenage pregnancy and childbearing, and, very recently, drug use—these remain serious problems facing today's teens. However, results . . . show that young people who have a close parent-child bond are most likely to avoid dangerous and destructive behavior. The challenge for families is finding ways of remaining connected while accommodating busy lives. The challenge for society is to complement parents' efforts by providing meaningful school and community activities for teens outside the home, and by insuring that families have the flexibility they need to spend time together.

Chapter Two

Parents who permit teens and their friends to drink at parties in their homes are asking for trouble. Young people can have a good time at a get-together without alcohol.

Helping Teens Make the Right Decisions

On New Year's Eve of 2002, 36-year-old Megan Smith allowed her 14-year-old daughter to hold a beer party at the family's home in Willow Grove, Pennsylvania. There were 25 ninth-grade students in attendance. During the party, Smith's 18-year-old son James allegedly sexually assaulted one of the girls. Megan Smith was arrested on charges of furnishing liquor to minors, endangering the welfare of children, and corruption of minors. James Smith was charged with statutory sexual assault.

In Lenexa, Kansas, 17-year-old Paul Riggs died when the pickup truck he was driving struck a tree on the way home from a beer party. Riggs' death prompted the Kansas state senate to adopt a law in March 2003 that made hosting underage drinkers a crime that could result in a six-month prison sentence for a guilty individual. In the fall of 2002, Judith McCloskey of Bangor, Pennsylvania, was sentenced to prison for this crime. After police learned that she hosted a party that led to the drunken driving deaths of three teenagers, she was charged with involuntary manslaughter.

John Morganelli, the district attorney who prosecuted McCloskey, explained the rationale behind the charge. He believed that although stopping kids from experimenting with alcohol is hardly feasible, going after the parents who make it easier is within the powers of the law. "That's why you're seeing a focus on adults as the facilitators of underage drinking," he said. "Our belief is that if adults stop doing that, it will be harder for kids to get the alcohol, and we might save lives that way." Concerned citizens like Rebecca Shaver, executive director of the Pennsylvania chapter of Mothers Against Drunk Driving (MADD), side with Morganelli and other prosecutors. "It's mind-boggling that any adult would think this is an OK thing to do, but I hear it all the time: 'I'd rather have my kid drinking at home,'" Shaver said. "I cringe when I hear that."

Mothers Against Drunk Driving, which lobbies for strict anti-drinking laws for young people, reported that 37 percent of 1,381 parents and 46 percent of 874 teenagers participating in a 2003 survey said they know of parents who host teenage drinking parties.

A Rebellious History

The above incidents of hosting beer parties represent the extreme lengths some parents will go to become involved in the lives of their teenagers. Most parents keep a reasonable distance; nonetheless, teenagers still find their parents involved in many facets of their lives. From the time most teenagers rise in the morning until lights out at night, parents stand as their main authority figures.

Parents set curfews, decide what their children eat, influence their decisions on whom to keep as friends, and play a major role in decisions about college. There is no question that teenagers often bristle at living on such short leashes. Adolescence is a time when young people start questioning authority and exerting their independence, insisting they make their own decisions.

In fact, teenage rebellion is hardly a new phenomenon, but rather has been a facet of American history for decades. Many of the same kids who sat at home in the early 1960s watching Wally and the Beaver dutifully obey their father later made history as one of America's most rebellious generations. During the 1960s teenagers questioned the authority of their parents, teachers, and political leaders, and helped launch the radical anti-Vietnam War movement that had swept across many college campuses by the middle of the decade.

Young people have a long tradition of activism in

Young demonstrators protest against the Vietnam War during a peace march in downtown Chicago, 1968. Young people have long been active in many causes, such as civil rights, anti-war efforts, and environmental protection.

the causes of civil rights, environmental protection, and the pursuit of international peace, which are often spawned by a healthy skepticism of what parents and other authority figures tell American youth.

In one of the most popular anthems of the 1960s, "The Times They Are A-Changin'," folk singer Bob Dylan sang, "Come mothers and fathers throughout the land / and don't criticize what you can't understand. / Your sons and daughters are beyond your command . . ." Nearly three decades later, hip-hop group Public Enemy rapped, "What we got to say / Power to the people no delay / To make everybody see / In order to fight the powers that be." The singers and the songs were different, but the meanings were very much the same.

In light of what has been accomplished through rebellious thinking, a teenager's independent attitude is not necessarily a bad thing. The challenge that parents face is to encourage teens to become independent thinkers while still making them understand the importance of adhering to the law and the tenets of acceptable moral behavior. Khalida Sims, a teenager from Cleveland Heights, Ohio, acknowledges her parents' role in trying to meet that challenge. "My parents always told me how to carry myself as a young lady," she told a reporter from *Ebony* magazine. "People are always looking at you no matter where you are, and you just have to carry yourself in an appropriate way because you are representing your family and everything that is a part of you."

Teen Sex and Abortion

The Gallup Youth Survey has often asked teenagers what sort of advice and guidance they receive from their parents. For example, in 2003 the Gallup Organization reported that 63 percent of the 13- to 17-year-old respondents who participated in its poll on sex education said their parents do talk to them about sex, while other respondents said they receive most of their sex education in school.

Many teenagers and their parents do maintain a healthy dialogue when it comes to sex. Colorado parent Karl Nicoletti told a news reporter in 2002 that he opened a dialogue about sex with his son Chris when the boy was in sixth grade.

"I know many parents who are wishy-washy when talking to their kids about sex," says Nicoletti. "I just said, 'No, you're not going to have sex . . . until you graduate from high school.'" Around the same time, Chris' future girlfriend, Amanda, had a similar conversation with her mother, Lynn. When the two

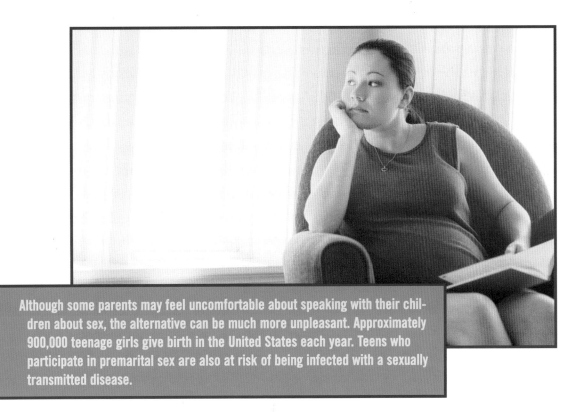

Although some parents may feel uncomfortable about speaking with their children about sex, the alternative can be much more unpleasant. Approximately 900,000 teenage girls give birth in the United States each year. Teens who participate in premarital sex are also at risk of being infected with a sexually transmitted disease.

teenagers began going out five years later, they promised their parents they would abstain from sex.

There is no question, though, that sex is one topic that many teenagers are most uncomfortable talking about with their parents. In fact, in a 1996 Gallup Youth Survey 20 percent of the respondents said they would like to discuss the topic of sex more with their parents, but 31 percent said their parents ask them too many questions about their sex lives. What many teenagers don't realize is that in the case of an unwanted pregnancy, their parents may have to become directly involved.

The U.S. Supreme Court legalized abortion in 1973 in the landmark *Roe v. Wade* decision. Since then, states have adopted laws regulating the procedure. One controversial issue that has required states to make additional regulations is teenage abortion. There are presently 43 states that require doctors and abortion clinics to notify parents when a teenage girl asks for an abortion.

States without parental consent laws include Washington, Connecticut, Hawaii, New Hampshire, New York, Oregon, Vermont, as well as Washington, D.C. Among the most restrictive states on this issue is Pennsylvania. Under the state's Abortion Control Act, a woman who requests an abortion must receive a mandatory counseling session from a physician and be accompanied by a parent. The doctor spells out the risks of abortion in this session, after which the woman must wait 24 hours and the parent must sign a consent form before she goes through with the procedure.

Setting an Example

Among the hot topics that Gallup Youth Survey asked teens about in 1999 was the night curfew. A total of 69 percent of the respondents said their parents set a school-night curfew for them, while 59 percent said they must also observe a weekend curfew. Of the teens who face curfews, 70 percent said that missing their curfew results in consequences, among which are being grounded, getting lectured, having to do extra chores, and losing car privileges.

Guidelines regarding nutrition and health habits have also been the topics of Gallup Youth Surveys. In 1999, a Gallup Youth Survey uncovered data suggesting that many parents who have been admonishing their teenagers to exercise, eat their vegetables, refrain from tobacco use, and get enough sleep are hardly setting good examples for their children to follow. The survey asked teens whether they practice a number of poor health habits and whether their parents practice those same habits. The results the survey found were alarming.

For example, 11 percent of the respondents said they smoke cigarettes and 41 percent said their parents smoke; 20 percent of the teens admitted to not getting enough exercise and 46 percent said they think their parents should exercise more. A total of 20 percent of the teens said they think they weigh too much and 39 percent said their parents probably weigh more than they should. Finally, 30 percent said they don't watch what they eat and 35 percent said they don't believe their parents watch what they eat.

One-quarter of the respondents said they don't get regular checkups by a physician and 32 percent believed their parents should be visiting a doctor more often; 9 percent of the teens said they drink more alcohol than they should, while 14 percent thought their parents drink too much. Regarding sleeping habits, 45 percent of respondents said they don't think they get enough sleep and 46 percent thought their parents could use more. Is it surprising that some teens have trouble listening to what their parents

Parents have a profound influence on their children. Studies indicate that many teens with bad habits like smoking may have picked up those habits from their parents.

have to say? Homes would likely see fewer instances of misbehavior if parents set better examples for their children.

Of all negative behaviors that teenagers may practice, none sets society on edge more than drinking alcohol. Despite the fact that none of the 50 states permits anyone to legally drink under the age of 21, many teenagers still find a way to gain access to alcohol even if their parents do not help them obtain it.

In 2001, 21 percent of the respondents to a Gallup Youth Survey said they drink alcoholic beverages. The same year the U.S. Centers for Disease Control and Prevention reported that 29 percent of young people have experimented with alcohol before the age of 13, and that 13 percent have driven a car after drinking. In addition, 30 percent of young people said they have ridden as passengers in cars they knew were driven by other young people who had been drinking. The death toll that has resulted from teenage drinking and driving is staggering. According to the National Highway Transportation Safety Administration, some 2,000 people between the ages of 15 and 20 die every year in alcohol-related car accidents.

Chapter Three

Laws that made it easier to get a divorce have contributed to a rise in the divorce rate since the 1950s. At that time, there were 5 divorces for every 1,000 married women. By 1978 the rate had risen to 23 divorces per 1,000 married women; today the rate has remained steady at about 21 divorces per 1,000 married women.

Irreconcilable Differences

In the spring of 2001, tabloid newspaper readers in New York City couldn't get enough of the bizarre story involving Mayor Rudolph Giuliani, his estranged wife, and his girlfriend.

Giuliani and Donna Hanover met in Miami, Florida, in 1982 and were soon married. By the time he was elected mayor of New York in 1993, Giuliani and Hanover seemed to be the ideal power couple—two strong-willed, influential, and successful people who were able to mesh their exciting careers with a healthy marriage. But by 1995, the marriage had gone sour, and by May 2001, the icy relations between Hanover and Giuliani had become very public and very embarrassing for Giuliani. Each day, there were new revelations in the press.

What was largely lost in all the media attention, though, is how the very public divorce between Rudolph Giuliani and Donna Hanover affected the couple's two teenage children,

Andrew and Caroline. The mudslinging between the mayor and his estranged wife became so heated that Acting Manhattan Supreme Court Justice Judith Gische finally stepped in and appointed a legal guardian to make sure the interests of the two children were cared for.

A High Divorce Rate

Most divorces do not, of course, end up on the front pages of tabloid newspapers, and in most cases judges do not have to appoint a guardian for the children. Nevertheless, the acrimony displayed by the two sides in the Giuliani-Hanover breakup is not uncommon. Chances are likely that the ill feelings between spouses about to divorce have festered for months, if not years. When things come to a boil, a divorce seems like the only solution to their problems. Sadly, though, divorce may not necessarily offer a solution to the problems that children will face in single-parent homes.

Divorce is quite common in American society. Roughly half the couples that get married in the United States get divorced. Because a large percentage of these couples have children, many teenagers live in a household with only one parent. In 83 percent of those cases, that one parent is the mother.

In recent decades divorce has reached epidemic levels in the United States. According to the National Center for Health Statistics, just 2 out of every 1,000 people were divorced in 1940. That number rose steadily, reaching a peak of 5.3 out of 1,000 people in 1977. Today, the rate has been reduced slightly, with roughly 4 out of every 1,000 people divorced.

There are some reasons for the slight drop in the number of divorced people in the United States. Members of the baby boom generation, a densely populated group of Americans born after World War II, are getting older. The majority of baby boomers are now in their 40s and 50s, well past the age when

There are about 12 million single-parent homes in the United States today.

most people consider getting a divorce. Also, although younger people are still living together, fewer are getting married. In the cases when they do split up, the separations do not count in the divorce statistics.

Despite this slight drop in divorce, the numbers are still staggering. According to the U.S. Census Bureau, there were some 12 million single-parent homes in the United States in 2000, representing about 32 percent of all family households with children. A total of 10 million of those homes were headed by mothers, while about 2 million were headed by fathers. To see just how high the divorce rate has grown, compare those numbers with statistics released by the U.S. Census Bureau just over 30 years ago. In 1970,

TEENAGERS STILL BELIEVE IN MARRIAGE

With so many marriages ending in divorce, it is tempting to predict a dismal future for the institution of marriage. But while the future is uncertain, study result indicate that young people are not as pessimistic as one might expect.

According to the Gallup Youth Survey, most young people expect to get married themselves and raise children. Since 1977, the Gallup Organization has asked them the following question: "Do you think you will get married some day or do you think you will remain single?" Over the years, more than 80 percent of the respondents have said they do plan to get married. In 2001, 93 percent of the 501 teens who were asked said they plan to get married, and 91 percent said they intend to have children.

Author and teacher Marline Pearson reached positive conclusions about the effects of marriage education in a study commissioned by the National Marriage Project, "Can Kids Get Smart About Marriage?" She stated that schools that are starting to offer such there were about 3 million single-parent households, representing about 11 percent of all family households with children.

The skyrocketing divorce rate can be attributed in part to the decisions by state legislatures to adopt so-called "no-fault" divorce laws in the 1960s and 1970s. In the years since this legislation was passed, it has been easier for husbands and wives to divorce, because they need no other reason than the declaration of "irreconcilable differences" to obtain legal separations.

This divorce process has been shed of many inconveniences, although the separations have still taken their toll on American children. In 2001, the Gallup Youth Survey found that just 56 percent of American teenagers live with both biological parents. And *Divorce* magazine reported that the total of children living with a divorced parent grows by a rate of one million a year and that in

instruction are making a difference in how young people view and respect marriage:

> Increasingly, public officials are turning to marriage and relationship education as one way to strengthen marriage and prevent divorce. Florida is the first state in the nation to require a course in relationships and marriage for all high school graduates. Elsewhere in the nation, teachers and others who work with school-age children are incorporating units on healthy relationships into existing curricula or offering marriage and relationship courses as electives.

In addition, the U.S. Census Bureau has found that people are waiting longer before getting married. According to census reports, the average age of marriage is now 27 for men and 25 for women—an increase of some five years for both genders since the 1960s. Facing less pressure to marry at an earlier age, many young people feel they have the time to wait until they are emotionally and economically prepared to make the commitment.

1998, some 20 million children under the age of 18 were living with just one parent. This segment represented 28 percent of all American children.

Over the years, psychologists have published many studies pointing out the emotional and economic impacts that divorces have on children. While there is basic agreement among mental health professionals that children of divorced parents face issues that other children do not, there are differing viewpoints on divorce's long-term impacts. There is no question, though, that children of divorce must face some very real life changes following the breakup of their parents' marriage.

The Single-Parent Home

In most cases, single-parent families are forced to live on a reduced income. Mediate.com—an Internet site maintained to serve attorneys and professional mediators who resolve divorce cases—reports that 60 percent of the people who live below the poverty level are divorced mothers and their children. According to Mediate.com, the average single mother may support up to four children on a paltry after-tax average income of $12,200 a year.

Many divorced fathers already help their families out of a natural sense of obligation. Other fathers fulfill their duty after a court orders them to pay child support—a monthly sum designated to assist families with expenses. Yet another group neglect families completely. Sometimes fathers are still at odds with their ex-wives, and they retaliate by withholding child support. In some unfortunate cases, they totally abandon their families. The courts will step in and order fathers to make their support payments, but legal proceedings are often slow, and deadbeat fathers—particularly those hard to track down—can get away without paying for months and often years. According to Mediate.com, 65 percent of all divorced mothers receive no child support at all.

The court faces limitations in enforcing child support, which means that many children have to adjust. For a teenager with a parent who is withholding support, there is sure to be less spending money and other amenities. He or she may have to find a part-time job to help meet the family's expenses. This added burden to work may be handled in time, though the emotional impact of divorce usually entails a much longer period of adjustment.

A study published by the National Institute of Mental Health charted the effects of divorce on teenagers' behavior:

> Children who grow up with two parents do better in many ways than children who grow up with only one. For example, children from one-parent homes have lower intellectual test scores and are more likely to drop out of school. Girls from such families are more prone to become single mothers in their teens, and boys are more prone to engage in antisocial behavior. These differences are seen in children from many social classes and ethnic groups.

A typical reaction by a teenager to divorce is the fear of being isolated and lonely. Young people may perceive that their parents are no longer available, and they may also feel as if they are being hurried into achieving independence. Some teenagers may even feel that they are now in competition with their parents.

Another possible reaction of teenagers is they will worry about their own future relationships and whether they will end badly like their parents' marriages. Teenager Kristina Herndobler from Benton, Illinois, whose parents divorced when she was four years old, offered her future expectations to a reporter: "I don't want my kids to wind up in a single-parent situation. And I don't want to have kids with a man I don't want to be married to forever. I don't believe in the fairy tale. I hope it exists, but I really don't believe it does."

Yet another response teenagers may have is a feeling of unease when their parents start dating again. Finally, teenagers may find themselves experiencing chronic fatigue and difficulty concentrating—both symptoms of depression. "I've always been anxious and never had much confidence," said Marta, a college freshman to an interviewer from the National Institute of Mental Health. "College was harder than I expected, and then my parents divorced, which was traumatic for me. After a while, all I did was cry, sleep, and feel waves of panic."

Making the Decision to Divorce

Divorce has become such a common thing that most teenagers wonder whether American parents are making the right decisions to separate. Over the years, the Gallup Youth Survey has asked teens, "Generally speaking, do you think it is too easy, or not easy enough, for people in this country to get divorced?" In 2003, a total of 1,200 teens between the ages of 13 and 17 were polled on that question, and 77 percent of the respondents said they believed it was too easy to get divorced.

The Gallup Youth Survey also asked teens, "Generally speaking, do you think that most people who get divorced have tried hard enough to save their marriages, or not?" In 2001, just 40 percent of the respondents believed that divorced people try hard enough to save their marriages.

The trials of divorce are very difficult for everyone involved. There may be a custody fight, in which the parents battle over whom the children will live with. Parents may also fight over the amount of child support or the distribution of the family's assets. If they can't resolve these issues between themselves, it is likely that they will hire lawyers and go to court. According to

Mediate.com, the cost of a litigated divorce in the United States can be as high as $35,000.

Family mediation specialist Kathleen O'Connell Corcoran explained the consequences of this litigation in a 1998 article for Mediate.com. "The focus is on assigning blame and fault and skirmishing for the most powerful position (changing locks, freezing bank accounts, getting temporary custody of the children)," she wrote. "Communications between parties break down. Negotiations proceed through attorneys and are strategic and positioned.

Teens whose parents are going through a divorce may feel very alone. During this turbulent time, they may not know which parent they can turn to for help with their own problems.

TEEN VIEWS ON DIVORCE

Do you think it is too easy or not easy enough for people in this country to get divorced?

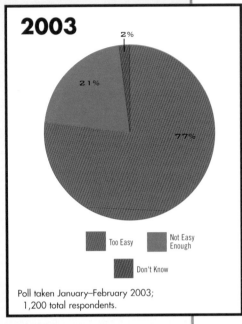

2003

2%

21%

77%

Too Easy

Not Easy Enough

Don't Know

Poll taken January–February 2003;
1,200 total respondents.

% saying "too easy"

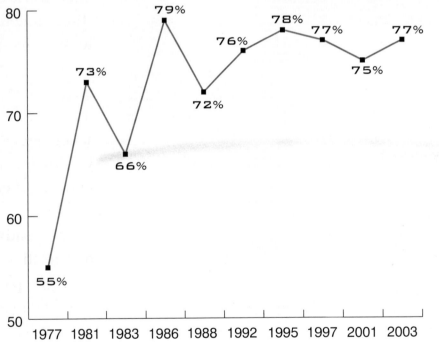

80

79%

78%

77%   77%

76%

73%

75%

72%

70

66%

60

55%

50

1977 1981 1983 1986 1988 1992 1995 1997 2001 2003

Polls taken between 1977 and 2003.
Source for both graphs: Gallup Youth Survery; The Gallup Organization.

Attorneys have an ethical responsibility to zealously advocate for the best interests of their client. Often there is no consideration of the best interests of the children or recognition for the need for parties to have an ongoing relationship because they have children, friends, extended family, and community together."

That fight over the family's assets may lead to the sale of the house. That means teenagers may have to move out of neighborhoods in which they grew up into strange new homes that will likely include smaller living accommodations. Perhaps teenagers who had their own room in the family's old house will find themselves now sharing a room with their little sibling, which means there is less living space for everyone in the family.

Even for teenagers lucky enough to stay in their old homes, things will be a lot different. The major difference is that one parent, usually the father, won't be coming home after work each evening. Instead, most children will typically see their fathers on weekends; a typical arrangement is for them to stay in their father's new home and return to their mother's on Sunday nights.

This arrangement is known as shared custody, which has proven to be a positive setup for children. For example, if the father is only seeing his children on weekends, chances are likely that he will make sure he spends quality time with them. Also, parents may remarry, and many young people will develop good relationships with their new stepfathers and stepmothers.

On the other hand, shared custody may also have its disadvantages. If parents continue to have an acrimonious relationship following the divorce, the occasions when the children are picked up can be awkward and tense. Parents may use the children to relay nasty messages to one another. Sadly, this puts the child in the middle. And while young people can develop good relationships with

Unfortunately, children whose parents are divorced, or going through a divorce, are often put in an awkward position between two people they love.

stepparents, there are many who find it impossible to get along with them. A report issued by the National Institute of Mental Health stated: "When a new spouse is brought into an ongoing parent-child relationship, relations with the stepparent do not generally resemble those between parents and children in nondivorced families; typically, stepparents offer less affection, interaction, supervision, and assistance."

Long-Term Effects of Divorce

Families are concerned with the long-term and as well as the short-term impacts of divorce on children. Psychologist Judith Wallerstein is convinced that long-term impacts are clearly evident. After interviewing children of divorce in the early 1970s, she stayed in touch with them for 25 years, and in 2000 she finally published the results in her study *The Unexpected Legacy of Divorce*. While she found many of her subjects were adjusting well as adults, she concluded that, overall, "whether the final outcome is good or bad, the whole trajectory of an individual's life is profoundly altered by the divorce experience."

One typical case that Wallerstein observed was a woman from Chapel Hill, North Carolina, whom the author refers to as simply "Karen" to keep her anonymous. According to Wallerstein, Karen found professional success but was unable to make a personal commitment to a relationship until the age of 34, when she had finally decided to get married.

"You remember that when I was dating guys in college, I became very frightened that anyone I really liked would abandon me or be unfaithful, and that I would end up suffering like my mom and dad?" Karen said. Wallerstein pondered the consequences of the decision to divorce, and how this particular split influenced Karen's views on long-term relationships: "Did her parents have any idea of what they had started 25 years ago when they filed for divorce? If they had known the long-term consequences for their children, would they have done things differently? Would they have divorced?"

Other mental health professionals disagree with the line of thinking that divorce continues to haunt young people well into their adult years. Says Penn State University sociology professor Paul Amato: "What most of the large-scale scientific research shows is that although growing up in a divorced family elevates the risk for certain kinds of problems, it by no means dooms children to having a terrible life. The fact of the matter is that most kids from divorced families do manage to overcome their problems and do have good lives."

The current research indicates that most children whose parents divorce do not drop out of school. They graduate, go on to college, launch successful careers, and get married themselves. Experts argue that it is not necessarily the number of parents that makes a difference in young people, but the quality of parenting they receive. Just because parents aren't living together doesn't mean they stop being parents.

Dr. Benjamin Spock, a pediatrician whose landmark book *Dr. Spock's Baby and Child Care* has not been out of print since it was first published in 1945, made the following observations on the subject of single-parent families:

I have stressed the importance of children's relationships with both their mother and father. But what if, as is commonly the case, there is only one parent at home . . . ? Must the child's psychological well-being inevitably suffer?

The answer to this question is a resounding no. While it is true that children need both male and female role models, those role models need not live in the same house. What children need most of all is nurturing and love, a consistent presence in their lives who provides emotional support and teaches them the ways of the world. A child growing up with a single parent who can provide these necessities will be far better off than a child whose mother and father neglect his needs because of their own unhappiness. Most children from single-parent families find role models outside the home—a special uncle or aunt, perhaps, or a close friend of the family.

We have learned that children are resilient: give them what they need and they will blossom. It is the necessities of love, consistency, and care that come first in a child's life. With those in hand, a child can do well in all sorts of different family constellations.

Chapter Four

A father and son spend quality time together. In general, dads spend much more time with their children today than their own fathers spent with them a generation ago.

Superdads

In the 1979 movie *Kramer vs. Kramer*, Dustin Hoffman plays Ted Kramer, a self-centered advertising executive who puts his career before his family. One day he arrives home from work to find his wife, Joanna (played by Meryl Streep), preparing to walk out on him. She gives Ted sole responsibility to care for the couple's six-year-old son, Billy, whom he has hardly taken the time to get to know.

The responsibilities of fatherhood hit Ted Kramer right in the nose. Suddenly, he realizes he doesn't know how to do even the simplest tasks for his son, such as making him breakfast. Slowly, though, Ted improves his parenting skills and develops a truly close relationship with his son. The story reaches its climax as Ted loses a court battle with his ex-wife. The judge awards custody of Billy to Joanna, but afterwards she realizes how close Ted and Billy have become, and decides to let the boy to remain in his father's care.

Kramer vs. Kramer was an enormously successful film, receiving widespread critical praise and earning five Academy Awards,

THE MILLION MAN MARCH

In 2000 the U.S. Census Bureau reported that 3 million black women are single mothers, and that they make up roughly 30 percent of all single parents in the United States. The census also reported that some 1.3 million single black mothers live below the poverty line. Given the fact that African Americans make up just 12 percent of the national population, it is clear that many fathers in the black community are not meeting their responsibilities to their families.

Certainly, there are many dedicated African American fathers who coach Little League teams, serve in Parent-Teacher Associations, and handle their baby-watching duties. Nevertheless, for years African American leaders have been troubled by statistics that revealed how many black fathers were simply walking away from their families. In 1995 Louis Farrakhan, leader of the Nation of Islam—a black religious sect of the Islamic faith in the United States—called for a million African American men to gather in Washington, D.C., as a demonstration of their solidarity, their concern with issues facing blacks, and their commitments to their families.

Farrakhan called the event the "Million Man March." It was staged on October 17, 1995, and although it drew fewer than a million men— the National Park Service estimated attendance at 400,000—there is no question that the march inspired many black men to recommit themselves to their families. "[P]eople came together to share solidarity for our own race," said Darius Smith of Baltimore, Maryland, who attended the rally with his son. "Now we must go out and do the task. We must go ahead."

Many black women supported the march and believed it was a great idea. "I think it's completely appropriate," said Nicole Ellis, a female law student at the University of Maryland who watched the Million Man March from the sidelines. "The uniting of these men is relevant including Best Picture. The film told the story of how Ted Kramer strives to become the type of father every child needs: one who participates wholly in his child's life. He spends time at home changing diapers, coaching Little League, meting out discipline when necessary, handing over the car keys, giving the right

to women because these are our fathers, and our sons. Black women already have a sisterhood among each other and this is really needed among black men."

The rally was held amid some controversy. In the past Farrakhan has ignited hatred among the races by making anti-Semitic remarks. For that reason, many black leaders—including future Secretary of State Colin Powell—elected to stay away from the Million Man March. Interviewed by a news reporter the day of the march, Powell said, "While I deplore the message of Minister Farrakhan, I cannot ignore what's happening in the presence of several hundred thousand African-Americans who care about themselves, care about the future, care about the future of this country."

Speaking from Austin, Texas, on the day of the rally, President Clinton said the Million Man March is all about "the frank admission that unless black men shoulder their load, no one else can help them or their brothers, their sisters, and their children escape the hard, bleak lives that too many of them still face."

A year after the rally was staged, several black leaders were asked whether they believed the Million Man March had truly ignited a sense of responsibility in black men who had previously failed to provide for their families. Armstrong Williams, a radio talk-show host and former staff member of the U.S. Equal Employment Opportunity Commission, commented on what other black men told him: "I talked to a lot of men who were not participating in the rearing of their children and as a result of the march, they've gone back home, not necessarily back with the mother of their children, but they pay child support, taking time with their sons and daughters."

advice—and still finds time to carve out a career for himself so that he will provide an adequate income for his family. In other words, a "Superdad."

Actor Paul Reiser, who wrote about his experiences as a new father in his memoir *Babyhood*, explained how he went through a life change not too far removed from Ted Kramer's:

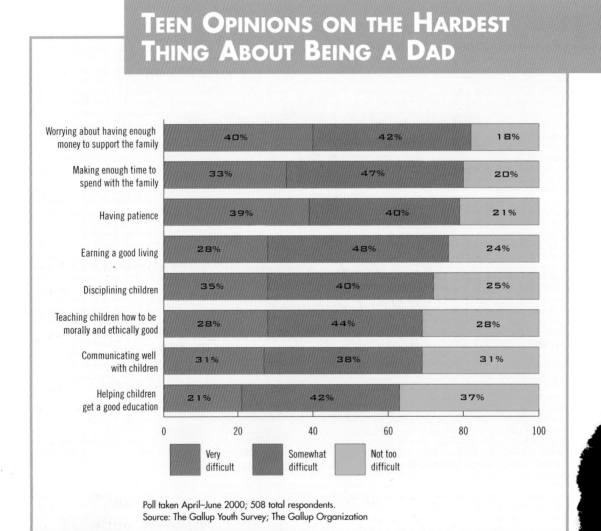

TEEN OPINIONS ON THE HARDEST THING ABOUT BEING A DAD

	Very difficult	Somewhat difficult	Not too difficult
Worrying about having enough money to support the family	40%	42%	18%
Making enough time to spend with the family	33%	47%	20%
Having patience	39%	40%	21%
Earning a good living	28%	48%	24%
Disciplining children	35%	40%	25%
Teaching children how to be morally and ethically good	28%	44%	28%
Communicating well with children	31%	38%	31%
Helping children get a good education	21%	42%	37%

Poll taken April–June 2000; 508 total respondents.
Source: The Gallup Youth Survey; The Gallup Organization

Having a baby dragged me, kicking and screaming, from the world of self-absorption. Now, I say to myself: "I know you want to sit down, but you can't. I know you want to go away for the weekend, but you can't." There are times of feeling resentful and moments when, quite honestly, I don't want to wake up at that hour of the morning. But you get past that and realize you have to let go of what you think you want.

In 2000, the Gallup Youth Survey asked teens a series of questions about what they thought of fatherhood. As much as 60 percent of the respondents said it is more difficult to be a father now than it was 20 or 30 years ago, and 82 percent said they felt the pressure on their fathers to earn enough money to support the family was "very difficult" or "somewhat difficult." A majority of the participating teens—80 percent—also said they felt that the pressure on fathers to make enough time to spend with their children was either "very difficult" or "somewhat difficult."

The reality of fatherhood is that most dads fall somewhere in between the type of father Ted Kramer was and the type he eventually becomes. In other words, Superdads are rare, though in recent years many fathers have made some initial steps forward. Recent studies may have shown that American fathers on average spend a mere 45 minutes a day caring for their children by themselves—in contrast to the average 10 hours a day a typical American mother spends—yet this is still an improvement from before. "Women are still doing twice as much [child care] as men, although 20 years ago they were doing three times as much," says James A. Levine, director of the Fatherhood Project of the Families and Work Institute. "Progress has been slow, and it will continue to be slow."

The Father's Role Changes

For decades—particularly in the 18th century and the early 19th century—fathers were the unquestioned authority in

American homes. Their influence on their children, particularly on their sons, was immeasurable.

In those days, children spent little time in school—usually just a few months every winter when the ground was frozen and it was too cold to grow crops on their farms. Once spring rolled around, though, the children—especially the boys—were needed to help in the fields. Boys spent all day working side by side with their fathers, who taught them values usually gleaned from the Bible. If fathers were industrious, pious, and dedicated to their families, then their sons were likely to mature into men with similar values. "The father was also the educator," says Michael Lamb, a psychology professor at the Catholic University of America in Washington, D.C. "It was his job, more so than the mother's, to instill values in his children."

That way of life largely changed in the mid-19th century as the Industrial Revolution took hold in the United States and major cities began to expand. Now, fathers left in the morning for jobs in factories and didn't see their children again until suppertime. Their role as family breadwinner became more prominent.

The 1960s was a period of great social change that initiated further adjustments to the father role. Fathers began playing a more supportive part in the childbirth process, for example. For the mothers using a newly developed method of childbirth known as Lamaze, fathers now were personal coaches. At home, they began looking after children during their infancy, performing tasks like changing diapers. Anyone who doubts the diaper-changing skills of fathers need only look in the men's rooms of the nation's airports and other public buildings—most now come equipped with diaper-changing tables.

The Fatherless Home

Although fathers have generally become more involved, there are still an inordinate number of fatherless homes. It is estimated by the National Center for Fathering that some 30 percent of all children are born outside of marriage; in many cases there is no father to help guide the mother through labor, or strap the baby into the car seat for the ride home from the hospital. She may go through the pain of labor alone, and if no family members come to her aid, she may also go through the child-rearing process alone. David

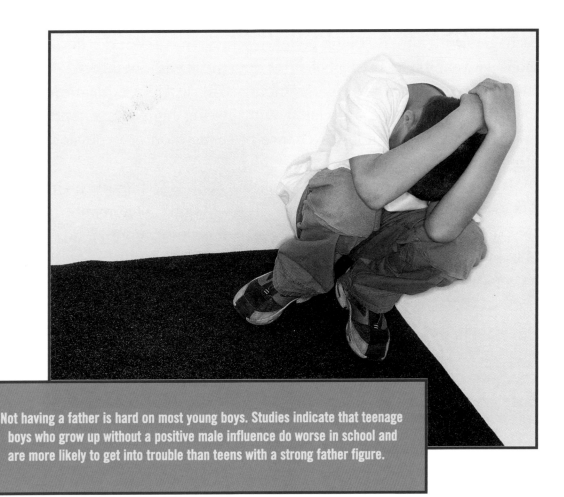

Not having a father is hard on most young boys. Studies indicate that teenage boys who grow up without a positive male influence do worse in school and are more likely to get into trouble than teens with a strong father figure.

Blankenhorn, author of the book *Fatherless America*, identifies "fatherlessness" as "the most destructive trend in our generation."

Children of fathers who have abandoned the home deal with a number of difficult issues. Many of those same issues confront young people who never experience life with a father. However, this is not a fact that adolescents are likely to admit to: results of a Gallup Youth Survey released in 2002 indicated that 41 percent of the 500 respondents felt the lack of a father had no effect on whether boys get into trouble.

Teenagers learn to make independent decisions without their fathers during adolescence; nonetheless, studies have shown that teenagers with fathers still do better in school, make sounder decisions, and exhibit less-risky behavior than those without fathers. A higher level of father involvement, said a U.S. Education Department study, "is associated with getting high grades and enjoying school, and a lower chance of suspension or expulsion from school."

It is generally rare to find teenagers who don't think their fathers figure importantly in their lives. Maggie Geiermann, a teenager from Pinckney, Michigan, explained to a reporter how she renewed bonds with her father. "My father is strict and hard to get along with," she said. "But he offered to drive me to school, and we started talking—about school, parties, our lives. He really opened up, and I saw a different side of him. . . . We have a special bond now." Jennifer Hollander of Nashua, New Hampshire, said she finds it hard to talk to her father about some issues, particularly sex. Nevertheless, she said, "I know if I really needed to, I would feel comfortable going to him."

When children are young, their fathers may change their diapers, teach them to ride bicycles, or coach their Little League teams. When children grow into adolescents, fathers establish college funds, give driving lessons, or show them how to run the lawn mower. Certainly, mowing the lawn in the 21st century bears little resemblance to helping to harvest the family's crops in the 19th century; nevertheless, the lessons that dads teach generally remain the same: doing a good job, taking pride in one's work, respecting one's property.

In his 1986 bestseller *Fatherhood*, comedian and educator Bill Cosby encouraged fathers to remain attentive to their children, particularly during the early adolescent years:

> Even though your kids may not be paying attention, *you* have to pay attention to them all the way. And if you really pay attention to them from the very beginning, then you'll know the moment they start to swallow or sniff things that rearrange their brain cells. . . . And with the attention, of course, must be all the love you can give, especially in the first 12 or 13 years. Then, when the kids start doing strange things under the guise of independence, they will always know that they are loved and that the lines are always open for them to send a message back to earth.

Chapter Five

Grandparents are playing a greater role in the raising of children than ever before. According to recent census data, grandparents are the heads of 7 percent of all households with children under age 18.

Unconditional Love

For an increasing number of Americans, the news that they will be parents comes most unexpectedly. For Mildred Horn, she found out at 5 A.M. on a May morning in 1985. She answered a knock on the door of her suburban New York home to find a policeman waiting outside. It was his sad duty to inform Horn that her daughter Hetty, a divorced mother of two children, had died in a car accident. At the time, Horn was 52 years old and a widow herself. When her former son-in-law decided not to claim custody of his children, Mildred became their new mother.

"It wasn't easy at first, but we found our way," Horn told a reporter in 1998. "The best part was that no matter how tired I was, one grandchild would always say, 'Oh, I love you Bubby.'"

Debbie Richardson developed a similar bond with her grandson, only under different circumstances. She and her husband, Dave, were struggling to deal with their out-of-control teenage daughter, Nikki. "There was drinking, drugs and sex. You name it," her mother, Debbie Richardson, told a reporter in 2001. "We would find empty cups under her bed that smelled like alcohol."

In 1996, Nikki graduated from high school in Louisville, Kentucky. She went to a commencement party and then disappeared for five days. When Nikki returned home, she announced to her mother and stepfather that she was pregnant. For Dave and Debbie Richardson, that was the final straw. "I made the biggest mistake of my life," Debbie Richardson said. "I threw her out."

Nikki moved in with her boyfriend and his parents, but just two weeks before her child was due to be born, she had a fight with her boyfriend and he kicked her out. Reluctantly, the Richardsons took her back, but Nikki's wild ways didn't end after she gave birth to a baby boy named Caley.

Although she was a devoted mother at first, Nikki soon slipped back into the party life and developed a cocaine habit. Finally, after Nikki disappeared again, Dave and Debbie Richardson contacted the local child services agency. The Richardsons then initiated legal proceedings to adopt the boy. The process became final in 1999 when Nikki agreed to forfeit her parental rights over Caley. Just three years before, the Richardsons had been looking forward to an easy life of retirement and the opportunity to travel; now their lives were controlled by the needs of a little boy. These grandparents had become parents once again.

Taking Over for Their Children

The stories of the Horns and the Richardsons are not unusual. The U.S. Census Bureau reports that grandparents are heading nearly 7 percent of all households with children under 18. Some 4 million American children are being raised by their grandparents,

More than 4 million children in the U.S. are being raised by their grandparents, many because their parents have given up their responsibility.

a total that is nearly twice as high as it was in 1970.

Contrary to popular misconceptions, the majority of grandparents who raise grandchildren are not poor and struggling in inner cities, but live in suburban homes. People are realizing it is more common for grandparents of all races and backgrounds to deal with raising a grandchild. According to census data, just 670,000 of the 4 million grandchildren living with their grandparents reside in a home headed by the grandmother—additional evidence running counter to the prevailing stereotype of the black grandmother raising a child in the inner city.

As a result of death, drug use, divorce, and abandonment, many grandparents have been forced to take over the parenting chores that their own children couldn't perform. "This isn't what they planned," says Renee Woodward, coordinator of the American Association of Retired Persons' Grandparent Information Center. "But they care about these kids and want them to be safe."

There are two primary reasons for this new trend among grandparents. One, in recent decades Americans have become grandparents at younger ages, making them more capable of taking on parenting duties. The Census Bureau reports that in 2000, just 21 percent of grandfathers and 15 percent of grandmothers who maintained their own homes were 65 and older. In addition, 72 percent of grandfathers and 56 percent of grandmothers who maintained their own homes were employed, and 36 percent of all grandparents who live on their own are reported to be in excellent or very good health. The old stereotype of grandpa snoozing in the rocking chair simply isn't as prevalent anymore.

Two, grandparents are living longer. According to the U.S. Centers for Disease Control and Prevention, in 1930 the average life expectancy for an American was not quite 60 years; by 1950 that number had grown to 69, and by 2000 it had reached 77. Today, because they become grandparents at an earlier age and are living longer, grandparents have a better opportunity to develop long-lasting relationships with their grandchildren than in past eras.

A Grandparent's Role

Psychiatrist Arthur Kornhaber, who established the Foundation for Grandparenting, explains the unique role of grandparents: "They're like grand viziers, wise people on enduring issues like ethics and morals. In all the years of history, grandparents have delineated the tribe and supplied the big picture: What do we want? Where are we going? How do we want to be?"

Kornhaber says most grandparents are willing to provide unconditional love to their grandchildren. In other words, if they attend a grandson's baseball game they'll tell him how impressed they are with how well he played, even when that might not be the complete truth. "Their parents love them, too, of course," Kornhaber adds. "But when you parent a child, it's 'all my unfulfilled hopes and dreams.' A father says, 'I want my child to be smart in math so I'm gonna do this.' Granddad simply says, 'Wow, you're great in math!'"

Grandparents can have an enormous influence on the lives of their grandchildren. Many of them become involved from the time their grandchildren are infants. There is no question that young parents need help with babies, particularly if they are facing the demands of parenting for the first time. Grandparents have been through it all before, and they are usually more than willing to step in to help, giving advice on the baby's care.

The Foundation for Grandparenting wanted to find out

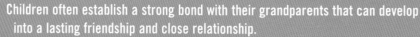
Children often establish a strong bond with their grandparents that can develop into a lasting friendship and close relationship.

through a study how children and adolescents feel about their relationships with their grandparents. Researchers interviewed several children between the ages of 5 and 18, who were divided into three categories according to the type of relationship they maintained with their grandparents.

Children with a close relationship with their grandparents generally believed that grandparents enriched their lives. They told interviewers that they felt "lucky" and believed their grandparents adored them. The second group was comprised of grandchildren who had been physically and emotionally separated from their grandparents. They told interviewers that they still felt attached to their grandparents, and were troubled that they couldn't see them more often. The third group had no contact with their grandparents, and said they felt something was missing from their lives.

"If [grandparents] establish a bond early, it will endure for life because grandparents never change form in a child's mind," Kornhaber said. "In fact, in young adulthood a good relationship is often rekindled. I've seen many kids actually take care of a beloved grandparent in a nursing home. The children wouldn't do it, but the grandchild will."

As grandchildren grow older and become more interested in the world around them, grandparents can provide a link to the past. They have a knowledge of family history that their children often lack. Grandparents' homes are often repositories for dozens if not hundreds of photographs of long-lost relatives, and grandparents can identify people in those pictures and explain their roles in the family's history. Carolyn Nell, a former president of the National Genealogical Society, explains why it is valuable for teens to know their family history: "By listening to the family stories, young people will not only gain a sense of identity, they'll also develop a personal sense of history that will help them in school."

Today's adolescent grandchildren are likely to have grandparents who grew up while the country was recovering from the

Great Depression of the 1930s. Their grandfathers may have fought in World War II or the Korean War. Teenage grandchildren are now hearing stories from those eras. In the years ahead, when today's teenagers start having children of their own, the stories those children hear will be a lot different. Future grandparents may tell them about their personal experiences fighting in the Vietnam War, attending peace protests in the 1960s, or even learning about the Watergate scandal that forced President Richard Nixon to resign in 1974.

In many cases grandparents are the lone religious educators in the family, either because parents have no commitment to a religion or are too busy to make sure their children make it to Sunday school or Hebrew school. When children start asking serious questions about difficult topics like where God lives or what he looks like, it often falls on grandparents to provide the answers. This was definitely the case with many grandmothers from Russia who immigrated to the United States during the second half of the 20th century. These women—the *babushkas*—kept the flames of Christianity burning in the former Soviet Union during the decades of official state atheism, and later instilled the values of the faith in their American grandchildren.

A Safe Haven

Adolescents who are frequently at odds with their parents often find the grandparents' home to be a safe haven from the daily trials with mom and dad. Grandparents may lend a sympathetic ear and give good advice. Certainly, grandparents can provide parents with an opportunity to take a break from their teenagers as well, which may help ease tensions for everyone. "When problems exist, an understanding, compassionate, nurturing and stress-free environment that grandparents can offer is just what teenagers need," explains Kornhaber. "[A] grandchild's problems can be respectfully heard, and advice can be freely given and received while watching a TV program together and eating popcorn, or on a drive to a sporting event or a shopping spree. And their parents

Grandparents can act as mediators between their children and grandchildren to ease family tension.

will appreciate knowing that the children are safe while things cool down."

A Gallup Youth Survey published in 2001 found that 93 percent of the 501 participating teenagers have living grandparents, and that 83 percent see their grandparents at least once a month. A slightly lower number — 79 percent — said they see their grandparents about five or six times a year.

In 1996, a Gallup Youth Survey reported that 11 percent of the respondents found it easier to talk things over with grandparents than with parents; 43 percent of the respondents said that on at least some occasions, they would rather talk over their problems with their grandparents before they approach their parents. The survey also reported that young teens — those between the ages of 13 and 15 — are more likely than older teens to rely on their grandparents as a sounding board.

As for the accounts of the Great Depression and World War II, 46 percent of the respondents in the 1996 poll said they enjoy listening to those stories a lot, while 30 percent said they are somewhat interested in the stories their grandparents tell. The remaining respondents said they have either little or no interest in the stories.

Grandparents buy their grandchildren clothes and baseball gloves, take them on fishing trips, start college funds, and make sure they have a few dollars in their pockets when they go back home. They may tell stories about their ancestors to their grandchildren and look after their spiritual education. They are also there for them when they need a break from mom and dad. And like Dave and Debbie Richardson, they may even be called on to take their grandchildren into their home and raise them as if they were their own.

In the end, the Richardson family survived its ordeal. Their daughter Nikki eventually straightened out her life. She gave up drugs, found a job, and gave birth to a daughter. Although she gave her son Caley up for adoption, she does visit him in her parents' home several times a month.

"Sometimes it hurts," Nikki told a news reporter, "but when I walk into a room and see [Caley and Debbie] hugging and kissing, it makes me smile. It makes me happy to know he's happy and he's got a good life."

Chapter Six

Two guests become involved in a hair-pulling fight during the taping of a *Jerry Springer* episode about family relationships. The crude subject matter, violent behavior, and obscene language of *The Jerry Springer Show* make it a target for criticism by those who believe the media must be more responsible.

The Push for Responsible Entertainment

When pop star Prince released his break-through album *Purple Rain* in 1984, 11-year-old Karenna Gore asked her mom to buy it for her. So Karenna's mom picked up a copy of the record, brought it home, and placed it on the turntable so she could listen to it with her daughter. When the needle arrived at the song "Darling Nikki," about a sex-crazed girl, Karenna's mother was appalled. "I couldn't believe my ears!" she said. "The vulgar lyrics embarrassed both of us. At first I was stunned—then I got mad!"

Karenna's mom happened to be Tipper Gore, wife of then-U.S. Senator Al Gore, who later became vice president of the United States. As it turned out, Tipper Gore wasn't the only wife of a powerful Washington political leader who was outraged by rock music lyrics.

Susan Baker, friend of Tipper Gore and wife of the secretary of the U.S. Treasury, James Baker, was also upset about the lyrics her children were

Two young children listen during a U.S. Senate hearing on the marketing of violent motion picture products to children, September 2000. Under pressure from government officials and parent groups, Hollywood executives have agreed to limit such practices.

STOP
MARKETING
VIOLENCE
TO
CHILDREN

hearing and the music videos they were watching. One day Gore and Baker learned they shared the same outrage and anxiety over the messages that the entertainment industry—particularly the music business—was sending to young people.

The two mothers and other Washington parents established the Parents' Music Resource Center (PMRC) to call attention to the lyrics of popular songs that they believed contained vulgar, sexually explicit, and violent messages. Soon, the organization began lobbying for new legislation that would demand the music industry to act more responsibly when it released songs with explicit lyrics or explicit music videos.

The PMRC held its first meeting at a church on May 15, 1985. The founders of the organization had only a vague notion that the public really cared about the issue they intended to raise. When 350 people showed up, Tipper Gore and the other PMRC organizers learned that their views on music lyrics reflected the feelings of many American parents.

At the time, the recording industry did not feel threatened by the PMRC's agenda, as no recording industry executives attended the first PMRC meeting. Soon, however, the recording industry found out more about the PMRC and how the organization intended to change the way rock music was marketed to teenagers.

Violence and Sex in the Media

Television. Music. Movies. The Internet. Video games. Teenagers have access to them all and are among the largest consumers of these forms of entertainment. For most of their waking hours, teenagers are bombarded with sounds and images from these entertainment outlets.

Reports have shown that at a time when parents and teenagers could be having meaningful conversations, they are also being distracted by the television. A 2002 report prepared for the National Institute on Media and the Family, based in Minneapolis, Minnesota, found that 58 percent of families with children have the television on during dinner. The report also discussed the implications of these numbers: "Presumably, this affects family interactions, in that this would be at a time when family members would usually talk to one another."

MANAGING MEDIA USE IN THE HOME

Many parents prefer not to be totally reliant on legislators and rating systems, and instead want to personally monitor what their children are exposed to in the media. One organization, the Media Awareness Network, serves parents in this regard. It recommends a number of ways parents and adolescents can work together to develop good viewing and listening habits. Among the things parents can do are:

Working with their children when they are young—even before they start school. Developing good media habits with children grows harder as they grow older.

Looking at their own media habits. Are they watching too much TV? Do they listen to songs with offensive lyrics? If parents have bad media habits it is important to change them before their children adopt similar habits.

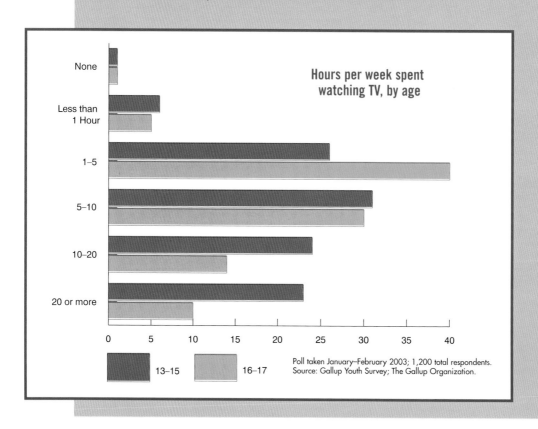

Hours per week spent watching TV, by age

13–15   16–17

Poll taken January–February 2003; 1,200 total respondents.
Source: Gallup Youth Survey; The Gallup Organization.

Finding other uses for their children's time instead of sitting in front of the TV and the computer screen. Parents can make sure their children's time is more devoted to sports, hobbies, or books.

Becoming involved in their children's media habits. It is important to watch TV with their kids, play their computer games, and listen to their records. They should also act as a guide when their children make choices about what to watch or what CDs to buy.

Becoming familiar with the various ratings and guides the entertainment industry has adopted.

It is very difficult for young people to avoid violent or sexually explicit images in the media, so when parents are watching a show or a movie with their children, it helps for them be prepared to talk over what their children have just seen.

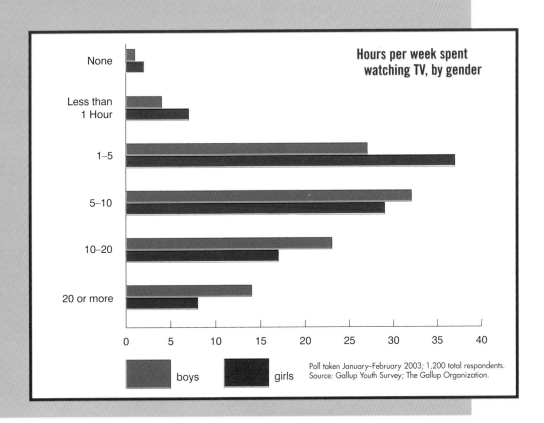

Hours per week spent watching TV, by gender

boys   girls

Poll taken January–February 2003; 1,200 total respondents.
Source: Gallup Youth Survey; The Gallup Organization.

Other statistics reveal how much time teenagers spend in front of the TV before and after dinner. In 2000 the Gallup Youth Survey polled 501 teenagers between the ages of 13 and 17, and learned that 67 percent say their parents put no restrictions on the number of hours they watch television. The U.S. Senate Judiciary Committee, which in 1999 investigated the exposure of violence in the media to young people, compiled the following entertainment-related statistics:

There is more than one television in 87 percent of American households, and almost 50 percent of children have television sets in their rooms.

Nearly 89 percent of homes with children have home video game equipment, a personal computer, or both.

An average American teenager listens to some 10,500 hours of rock music between the 7th and 12th grades.

By age 18, an American child will have seen 16,000 simulated murders and 200,000 simulated acts of violence.

The average seventh-grader watches about four hours of television per day, and 60 percent of those shows contain some violence.

The average seventh-grader plays electronic games at least four hours per week, and 50 percent of those games are violent.

Since that tragic day in April 1999, many residents of Littleton, Colorado, are aware of the troubling statistics about violence and electronic games. Eric Harris and Dylan Klebold, two disaffected teenagers who shot and killed 12 classmates and a teacher at Columbine High School before killing themselves, were devoted fans of the violent video game *Doom*. After the tragedy, some Americans found a correlation between Klebold and Harris' massacre and the scenarios in the game *Doom*, in which a space marine walks through hallways killing at will.

To further an understanding about the relationship between teen violence and entertainment, the Gallup Youth Survey has often questioned teenagers on whether they think the content of

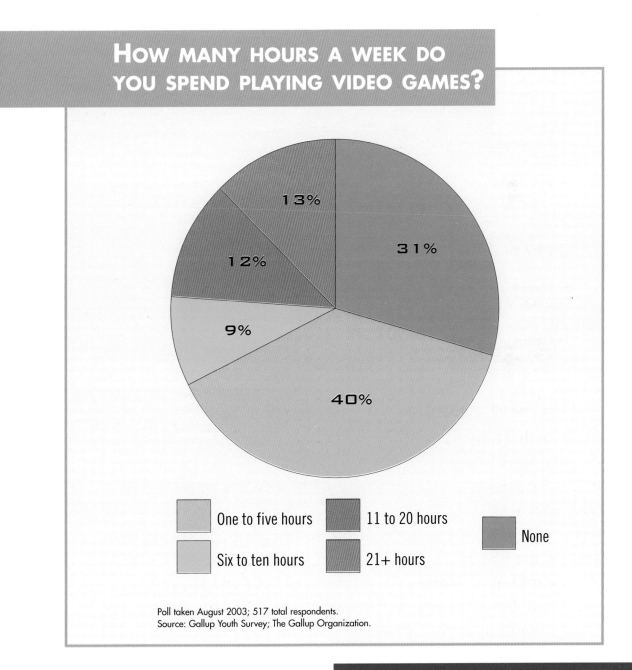

HOW MANY HOURS A WEEK DO YOU SPEND PLAYING VIDEO GAMES?

13%

12%

31%

9%

40%

One to five hours

Six to ten hours

11 to 20 hours

21+ hours

None

Poll taken August 2003; 517 total respondents.
Source: Gallup Youth Survey; The Gallup Organization.

THE HOLLYWOOD CENSORS

In 1930, the movie industry adopted a set of voluntary guidelines known as the "Hays Code," which regulated the content of films. Named after Will Hays, president of the Motion Picture Producers and Distributors of America, the code prohibited the production of movies that threatened to "lower the standards of those who see it." Certain situations in movies were deemed inappropriate and banned, such as homosexual unions or couples having children out of wedlock.

Hays maintained firm control over Hollywood, which continued to make sure films promoted positive attitudes toward marriage, family, home, the government, and religion. Censors working for Hays looked over scripts and were authorized to order rewrites if they felt the movies did not live up to the spirit of the Hays Code. Virtually no movie could be screened in a U.S. theater without the consent of these censors.

Of course, just because the censors wouldn't let films depict social ills in the United States didn't mean there weren't any. During the Hays era, unwanted pregnancies, sexually transmitted diseases, abortion, suicide, divorce, and child abuse were a part of American life, as they are today.

By the 1960s, the Hays Code had long since been forgotten. The 1960s was an era of turmoil in the United States, and the movies of the decade reflected the willingness of filmmakers to challenge the rules of what was regarded as acceptable film content. Films started depicting the type of social issues that Hays censors had banned, and now profanity, nudity, and sex were featured on screens in the United States.

Although the times were changing, films with explicit content still incited critics. Government leaders, educators, and parents' groups questioned whether the content of some films should be acceptable to all audiences. On some occasions censors felt the need to skirt the law. In 1968, U.S. Customs agents seized prints of a racy Swedish art film, *I Am Curious Yellow*, before they could be distributed to U.S. theaters. The Customs Service alleged that the movie's stark depictions of nudity and sex were obscene. A federal jury agreed with the Customs ban, but the decision was overturned on appeal and American theaters showed the film.

Following this court decision, filmmakers realized they would have to develop self-regulated guidelines or face similar court challenges to their work. In 1968, executives in the motion picture industry developed a film rating system that included the designations "G" for general audience, "R" for "restricted to viewers over the age of 17 unless accompanied by an adult," and "X" for "no one under 17 admitted at all." Over the years the ratings have undergone adjustments. Now the ratings include "G" as well as "PG," for "parental guidance advised"; "PG-13," for "some material may be inappropriate for children under 13"; and "NC-17," which replaced the "X" rating. In addition, the "R" rating now entails specific information regarding the movie's adult content, which could include violence, sex, nudity, drug use, or a combination of any of these elements.

Other entertainment media have been slow to copy the ratings system employed by the film industry, but most sectors of the entertainment business eventually found a way to balance the public's desire for a responsible media against the constitutional guarantee that artists can create their work in an uncensored environment.

The video game industry has acknowledged the need to keep parents informed through a rating system. Video games that are appropriate for younger players include the ratings "E," for games appropriate for "everyone," and "KA," which means the content is suitable for "kids to adult" but contains some mild violence and mature language. For older players, there are the ratings "T" for "teen"; "M" for "mature," which means the game should be played by people 17 years and older because it contains themes of intense violence and language; and "A" for "adults only."

The television industry has perhaps had the longest struggle to find a way to rate its content. At first, industry executives were willing to air mature programming late at night but still during the hours of "prime time," when networks can charge the most money for advertising. This stipulation meant mature programming was hitting the airwaves as early as 10 P.M.—a time when most teenagers were still tuned in.

Technological advancements during the late 1990s made it easier to restrict young viewers from seeing certain types of content. TV manufacturers could now install devices called "V-Chips" in televisions so that parents could program their sets to lock out specific shows, or all shows of a certain rating. Most television sets manufactured after January 2000 contain the V-chips.

TV ratings that pertain to the youngest audiences include "TV-Y," "TV-Y7," and "TV-Y7-FV," which means the content is suitable for older children but contains fantasy violence. The "TV-G" rating applies to content suitable for general audiences. For older audiences, there is "TV-PG," which means the content may be unsuitable for younger children; "TV-14," which warns parents that the programming contains material that may be unsuitable for children 14 years and younger; and "TV-MA," which means the programming can be viewed by adults only.

movies and other forms of entertainment are too violent or sexually explicit. Polls have shown that over the years a declining number of teenagers believe there is too much sex and violence in the movies. This decline has convinced many people that teenagers are becoming desensitized to what they see on the multiplex screens.

In 1977, the Gallup Organization asked 502 teens between the ages of 13 and 17 what they thought of violence in the movies. A significant number of the respondents—42 percent—said they believed there was too much violence depicted on movie screens; 22 years later, just 23 percent of the respondents said they thought movies were too violent. On the issue of sex in the movies, the gap between the time periods was similarly large: in 1977, 44 percent of the respondents agreed that there was too much sex; in 1999, just 28 percent said there was too much sex.

Over the years there have been hundreds of studies concentrating on violence in the media, and nearly all have concluded that exposure to violent images on TV, the movies, and other forms of entertainment encourages aggressive behavior in young people. What's more, studies on sex in the media have shown that teenagers get most of their ideas about sex from what they see on TV or the multiplex screen, or what they hear coming out of their stereo headphones. Usually, these depictions introduce few of the facts that young people should know before making decisions about sex, such as the fact that sex without contraception can lead to unplanned pregnancies and sexually transmitted diseases. Instead, movies, shows, and music videos often present situations in which sex is carefree and risky.

Sex is just as prevalent in the media today as it was some 20 years ago, when Tipper Gore and her daughter first heard Prince's lyrics. Many parents who are familiar with MTV wonder what they can do to keep such images off the airwaves: the answer is they can do little. Because the First Amendment guarantees freedom of speech and expression to writers and artists, Congress is usually careful not to infringe on these rights in the fields of art, music, cinema, and television. The courts have also consistently upheld the rights of creative people to express themselves.

Still, members of Congress and U.S. presidents have been firm in their convictions that the media should act more responsibly. The media have responded to a large degree. The Motion Picture Association of America (MPAA) has a review board that has imposed a rating system on its films since 1968. Participating theater owners have committed themselves to barring admission to anyone not meeting the minimum age guidelines. Other sectors of the entertainment media have also responded with self-rating systems.

Parental Advisory Labels and the PMRC

The recording industry, which was at first adverse to a parental advisory system, finally conceded and adopted a labeling system. After that first meeting of the Parents' Music Resource Center in the spring of 1985, the movement to make the recording industry accountable gained momentum. That fall, a subcommittee of the U.S. Senate held hearings on the constitutionality of putting parental advisory labels on albums that contained sexually explicit or violent lyrics. On September 19, the subcommittee heard testimony in a packed Senate hearing room. "The hearing certainly brought the issue out for public debate," recalled Tipper Gore. "It turned out to be the most widely publicized media event in congressional history. A seat in the hearing room was the hottest ticket in town all year."

Gore and Susan Baker testified on behalf of the PMRC. The organization suggested that in addition to the advisory stickers, the lyrics of all of the album's songs should be printed and issued with the record so that parents could read the lyrics. The standing-room-only crowd was drawn to the hearing to witness the testimony of some of the music industry's hottest recording artists. Dee Snider of the rock group Twisted Sister, country star John Denver, and art-rock composer Frank Zappa hoped to convince the senators that parental advisory labels represented a step toward censorship.

"I am 30 years old," said Snider. "I am married. I have a three-year-old son. I was born and raised a Christian and I still adhere to those principles. Believe it or not, I do not smoke. I do not drink, and I do not do drugs."

Twisted Sister had been singled out by the PMRC for the song "Under the Blade," which the parents' group said promoted rape. Another song by Twisted Sister, "We're Not Gonna Take It," was placed on the "Filthy Fifteen," a list of songs the PMRC claimed were particularly violent or sexually explicit. Other artists who found their songs on the list were Madonna, Def Leppard, Cyndi Lauper, and Black Sabbath—the group led by Ozzy Osbourne in the days before he became one of TV's best-known fathers.

Musician Frank Zappa testifies during a September 1985 Senate hearing about the constitutionality of putting warning labels on albums with explicit lyrics. Although the government decided not to pass legislation requiring the parental advisory labels, the recording industry voluntarily agreed to place the labels on the front of album covers.

The Senate committee elected not to recommend legislation requiring parental advisory labels or the publication of lyrics with albums. The senators believed they their decision protected the First Amendment rights of artists. In the end, Congress didn't have to pass legislation after all. In November 1985, the Recording Industry Association of America (RIAA), which represents most of the nation's major record companies, reached an agreement with the PMRC as well as the National Parent-Teacher Association to voluntarily publish lyrics and place warning labels on the front of album covers. The labels earned the nickname "Tipper Stickers."

Years later, RIAA President Hilary Rosen explained the rationale behind the agreement:

> The recording industry takes seriously our responsibility to help parents identify music with explicit lyrics. We believe that not all music is right for all ages and our *Parental Advisory Label* was created for just that reason. Parents can use the label to identify music that may not be appropriate for their children and make the choice about when—and whether—their children should be able to have that recording.

The Parent Movement Continues

After the PMRC showed that parents could make a difference in helping keep the music industry accountable, additional parents' groups formed to monitor other forms of entertainment. One such group is the Parents Television Council (PTC), which since it was established in 1995 has grown to more than 800,000 members. As its name implies, the PTC scrutinizes television programming and calls attention to shows that it does not believe are suitable for young people.

In satisfying its mission, one method the organization has employed is to target advertisers that show commercials during the programs deemed unsuitable for family viewing. One of the more well-known crackdowns occurred in 2002, when the PTC pressured 20 companies to withdraw advertising that aired during *The Shield*, a police drama on the FX cable network.

Because the show regularly featured explicit sex, nudity, obscene language, and violence, the PTC called on corporations like Burger King, Office Depot, Cingular Wireless, and Subaru to withdraw their advertising from the show, costing FX an estimated $26 million in revenue.

In 2002 L. Brent Bozell III, president of the PTC, expressed his satisfaction with the council's progress:

> When we launched the PTC over seven years ago, TV advertisers refused to take responsibility for what their advertising dollars put on television. No longer. The PTC has made a national issue of television sponsorship, making them accountable for the content of the programs they support with their ad dollars. Major corporations are hearing the message—loudly—and are shying away from programs with offensive content, and investing in wholesome fare instead.

Chapter Seven

This young student's mother is also her teacher. About 2 million children in the United States are educated at home each year.

How Parents Can Influence the Schools

At the Golden home in Austin, Texas, school convenes every morning in the family's living room. There the Golden children—Zachary, age 15; Rachel, 11; and Jacob, 5—report for classes. The children's parents, John and Beverly, are also their teachers, and their lessons cover subjects such as history, reading, foreign languages, and mathematics. Although some of the children have gone to public schools from time to time, for the most part the Goldens are "home-schooled."

Two older children, Gabriel and Judith, have already received instruction from the "Golden Academy" and have gone on to college. Judith, who finished up her secondary years at a public school, graduated in the top 5 percent of her class and majored in biology at the University of Texas, with plans to become a veterinarian. Gabriel, who went on to enroll in classes at Austin Community College, scored so high on a statewide math assessment that a counselor suggested he begin college immediately. At the time, he was only 16 years old. "Homeschooling is just an alternative," Beverly Golden told a news reporter. "We're always looking—is this the best way, is this the best year, is this the best thing for this kid?"

The Golden children are among the nearly 2 million American children who receive their education at home, according to the National Home Education Research Institute, a homeschool support group. Once unthinkable—and in most places, illegal—homeschooling is now permitted in all 50 U.S. states. Parents of homeschooled kids have made the decision to take full responsibility for the instruction of their children.

Although homeschooled students are much more common than they were 10 years ago, most young people still leave their homes each morning for class in public, parochial, or private schools. But while the majority of parents may not be directly responsible for their children's instruction, they are still involved in life at school, helping make decisions on what is taught in the classroom, as well as how much of the school budget is spent on books and materials, new desks, teachers' salaries, and nearly everything else that goes into the students' education.

Committed Parents

Parental involvement in schools has been a constant throughout U.S. history. In colonial times, parents were largely responsible for the schools, and in some cases they pooled their funds together to hire a schoolteacher. Often an itinerant clergyman arrived in town and announced that he was qualified to teach school and would do so for a teacher's modest salary, as long as the community provided him with pupils and a school building.

Today, parents do not build the schools themselves but they certainly pay to have them built. As taxpayers, parents as well as

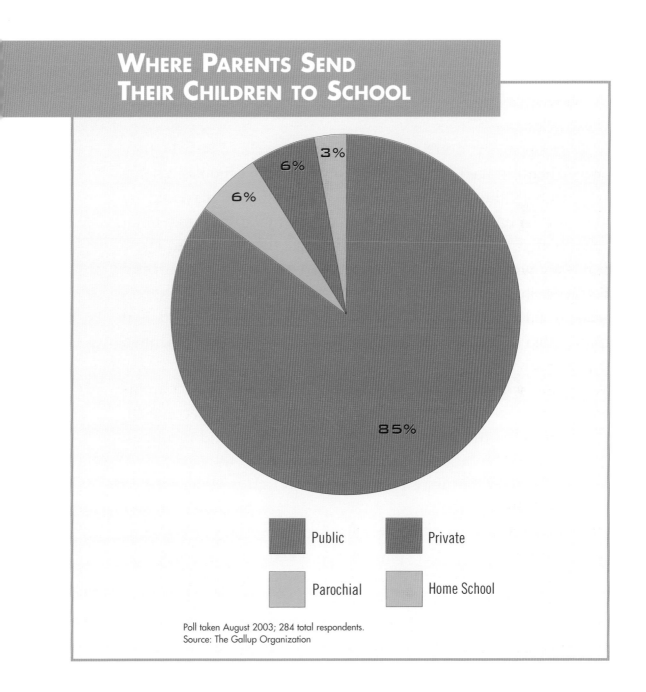

WHERE PARENTS SEND THEIR CHILDREN TO SCHOOL

6%

6%

3%

85%

Public

Private

Parochial

Home School

Poll taken August 2003; 284 total respondents.
Source: The Gallup Organization

other community members usually have a considerable influence on decisions about the school's location, size, and features. In many school districts, the question of whether to build the school may be placed before the voters in what is known as a referendum. Local voters may also elect school board members. It is not unusual for many parents to serve on school boards and make decisions that affect their children as well as all other students in the district.

Even if parents don't run for election on school boards, they are still encouraged to become involved in the schools in some way. In fact, the Improving America's Schools Act, passed by Congress in 1996, established a plan of parental involvement that schools had to implement to qualify for "Title I" funds. These funds are provided to school districts based on the number of students whose family incomes fall below the poverty line. Congress redefined the plan in 2002 when it passed the No Child Left Behind Act. Some 90 percent of all school districts in the United States receive Title I funds.

A school district's plans for Title I must show how parents can become active in the school's programs. Parents become eligible for Title I funds by attending school events and meetings. These funds can be used to pay for child care, transportation, and other costs that may be incurred through participating in the program.

Schools have reacted to the Title I rules by developing some innovative ways to get parents involved. For example, at Hazelwood Elementary School in Louisville, Kentucky, parents serve as library assistants. They also help to plan monthly birthday parties for students and volunteer for the school's Reading Is Fundamental program. During monthly Family Nights at the school, parents and students watch a short movie or listen to a storyteller, then talk over the lessons that can be learned from the presentations.

At the Signal Hill Elementary School in Long Beach, California, the school has developed a pledge that each parent is asked to sign. This kind of pledge has become common at many other schools. By signing the pledge, Signal Hill parents promise to do the following:

> Send their children to school appropriately dressed, prepared to learn, and on time.
>
> Read to their children at least 15 minutes a night.
>
> Attend at least one parent-teacher conference a year to discuss the academic progress of their children.
>
> Assist their children with their homework assignments on a regular basis to ensure completeness and accuracy.
>
> Volunteer at the school at least 10 hours a year.

Long before Congress passed acts that encouraged parental involvement, parents committed themselves to schools through Parent-Teacher Associations, which are still very active today. The National PTA dates back to 1897, when an organization called the National Congress of Mothers formed in Washington, D.C. The association was among the earliest advocates for physical education and sex education programs in schools, as well as the establishment of kindergarten classes, child labor laws, a juvenile justice system, mandatory immunizations, and hot lunches. Most of what the National Congress of Mothers advocated for has been legislated into law. The organization changed its name to the National Parent-Teacher Association in 1908.

Book Banning

Parental involvement sometimes goes beyond what the law prefers or what public-service organizations like the PTA have in mind. Parents may find themselves involved in school issues as they react to a course their child is taking, the selection of food in the school cafeteria, or a book they have found on their child's reading list.

Protests over assigned reading material or school library books have been common throughout U.S. history. Typically, parent groups find themselves of a similar mind on a book and band together to raise concerns in front of school boards. Administrators and school board members show sensitivity to the concerns raised by parents, and sometimes the chorus of complaints results in a ban on the book. Some of the more famous books that have been banned by schools in U.S. history are Mark Twain's *Adventures of Huckleberry Finn*, J. D. Salinger's *The Catcher in the Rye*, and Alice Walker's *The Color Purple*.

Authors, publishers, and librarians have been involved in constant battles with schools over book-banning issues. They maintain that the books in question raise important social issues that need to be exposed to young readers. In recent years, an author who has fought hard to keep her books on school library shelves is Phyllis Reynolds Naylor, who wrote a series of books that follow the maturation of an adolescent girl named Alice.

In 2002, the school board of Webb City, Missouri, heeded parents' complaints and removed three of Naylor's books—*Achingly Alice, Alice in Lace*, and *The Grooming of Alice*. In one scene of the series that particularly raised anxieties, Alice and her friends attend a school health class and a nurse shows them pictures of a female body, explaining how it changes through adolescence. Some parents believed that their children could be introduced to sex education and other sensitive topics in a different way. In response to the ban, Naylor countered that the parents "miss the point so much. I get letters from kids about book banning that say: 'Our parents have no idea what we think about. They still look at me as an innocent little girl or an innocent little guy.'"

Other school boards have also wrestled with the issue of banning books. Parents have complained about such books as the enormously popular Harry Potter series, claiming the books glorify witchcraft,

School libraries can become centers for controversy when parents are opposed to particular books, films, or other educational resources.

First-grade students get their lunches in a New Hampshire elementary school cafeteria. Some parents have criticized schools for selling snack food from vending machines, or foods that are high in fat such as pizza and hamburgers in the cafeterias.

and *Anne Frank: Diary of a Young Girl*, which as an account of the Holocaust has been considered too depressing for children.

Some educators believe that parents are being too protective of their students in banning these books. "We've had complaints about 'The Diary of Anne Frank' because it was, and I quote, 'a real downer,'" said Judith Krug, director of the Office of Intellectual Freedom for the American Library Association. "Well, yeah, I guess the Holocaust was a downer. But I think what Anne Frank had to say is extremely important in terms of teaching children what went on in that environment, and providing them with a historical document that still has some validity today."

In some cases administrators and school boards have stood up to parents and refused to ban books. In 1997, school administrators in Jefferson County, Kentucky, turned back requests by parents to ban three books by gay author E. Lynn Harris—*Invisible Life, Just As I Am,* and *This Too Shall Pass*—which all have characters who deal with their homosexuality.

Students, like 17-year-old Stacy Riger, have also argued to keep books on school reading lists. "I just don't think we can have a controlled, censored classroom," she said. "We definitely can't hide these different lifestyles from our young people by pretending they don't exist."

Junk Food in the Cafeteria

The school library isn't the only place where parents have cast a wary eye. Many parents have examined their children's school cafeteria and wondered whether it offers healthy food for them. What has particularly disturbed them is the presence of vending machines in many cafeterias. They question whether unhealthy soft drinks and snacks should be made available on school grounds. School administrators argue that the machines are a source of revenue that helps offset expenses.

"You could pretty well assume there's at least one if not two, three or four [vending machines] in every high school or middle school in the state," says Jim Ballard, executive director of the Michigan Association of Secondary School Principals. "This is how a good share of our school's extracurricular activities are funded. The student council, the chess club, the honor society, the debate club, the French club—this is where they get their funding. And that's critical to our schools."

There is no question that the snack sales do help fund school activities. According to the National PTA, some 350 school districts have signed contracts with vending machine or snack food companies that enable them to share in the profits from sales. One of the most lucrative contracts in the nation is held by the Santa Clara Unified School District in California, which earns as much as $400,000 a year in snack food and soft drink sales. Still, parents argue that snack foods and soft drinks are far from nutritious and that schools could find money-raising alternatives that don't promote obesity and poor dental hygiene.

"We've got so many kids who are diabetics," Michigan parent Diana Underwood told a reporter. "They're so overweight. Some of the things we do, like selling [soda] in the schools, it just rattles the brain." In many school districts, parents have lobbied hard to ban the sales of soft drinks and snack foods. They have had few victories, but nevertheless have raised awareness of the issue. Michigan legislator Virg Bernero, whose efforts to outlaw snack foods and soft drinks at schools have thus far been unsuccessful, does not buy the argument that vending machines are a good source of revenue:

> You could raise a lot of money selling cigarettes in schools. That doesn't make it right. Kids today drink twice as much soda pop as they do milk. That's exactly the opposite of what it was 20 years ago. When you look at the super-sized shape of a lot of kids today, when you look at the rise of Type II diabetes and obesity, pop is the single biggest offender. That's the reason I'm concerned about increasing the access by these companies to our children.

Sex Education

Most parents believe the classroom is an appropriate place for their adolescent children to learn about sexually transmitted diseases, contraception, pregnancy, and similar issues. The 2000 study

"Sex Education in America," sponsored by the Henry J. Kaiser Family Foundation, found that 65 percent of parents believe sex education in the schools should address contraception as a method to avoid unwanted pregnancies and sexually transmitted diseases. Still, sex education is one part of the curriculum that some parents have regularly questioned. One popular claim is that schools don't do enough to stress abstinence over contraception.

"There is no such thing as safe sex," parent Cathy Ponder told a news reporter in 2002. "Children deserve the truth, and they deserve to know that condoms do not protect you." Ponder was part of a parent movement that convinced the school board of Northville, Michigan, to make sex education an elective course.

In nearby Rochester, Michigan, a group of parents believed that an instructional videotape, *What Kids Want to Know About Sex*, was too explicit for 12-year-old students, and persuaded school administrators to shelve the tape. The video depicted a boy asking a physician frank questions about sex. Teachers in Rochester defended the movie, arguing that they hear their students raise many of the same questions in the school hallways and cafeterias and that the video could provide students with accurate answers.

Carolyn Mack, a mother of four Rochester students and member of a sex education advisory committee for the school district, stood up for the concerned parents: "To say this is the way it is and we parents have to acquiesce is a cop-out. These videos encourage experimentation. They teach kids to circumvent parents."

Homeschooling and School Evaluation

Of course, if parents disagree with how a school teaches sex education, or whether there are too many snack and soda machines in the cafeteria, or if they don't like the selection of books available on the library shelves, they have that option to pull their children out of school and teach them on their own.

That's what parents started doing in large numbers in the 1980s. Conservative Christians were among the first parents to turn to homeschooling. In many cases their decision stemmed from a desire to provide a religious education for their children. Under law, public schools are forbidden to hold religious services, teach Bible lessons, or in any way address the religious educations of their students. Although there are many private Christian schools that see to those needs, their tuitions are often too expensive for families. For these reasons many parents decided they would teach the Bible at home—along with arithmetic, history, and spelling.

The first roadblocks parents encountered were state laws prohibiting homeschooling, but organized lobbying efforts and court challenges soon overturned those laws. Soon many parents of Christian and other faiths joined the movement. Today homeschooling is legal across the United States, although many states do maintain specific rules about what is taught and how students are evaluated.

The National Home Education Research Institute estimates that overall, the ranks of homeschooled students grow by as much as 15 percent a year. Today there are a number of reasons why parents choose the homeschooling alternative. Some parents are concerned about crime and violence in the schools, others disagree with the curricula, and a third group simply does not think the schools do a very good job.

Whether schools are doing their jobs is a question that teens as well as parents have asked. In 2003, the Gallup Youth Survey asked 1,200 teens between the ages of 13 and 17 to evaluate their

How Students Grade U.S. Schools

Students often are given grades of A, B, C, D and fail on the quality of their work. What grade would you give your school?

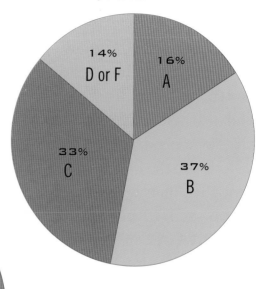

14%
D or F

16%
A

33%
C

37%
B

What would you grade the extracurricular activites available at your school?

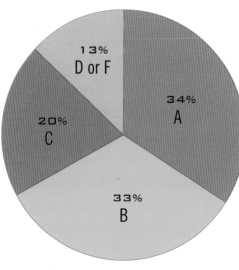

13%
D or F

20%
C

34%
A

33%
B

What would you grade the technology available at your school?

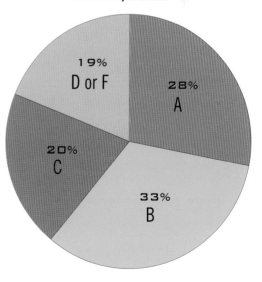

19%
D or F

28%
A

20%
C

33%
B

Poll taken January–February 2003; 1,200 total respondents.
Source: Gallup Youth Survey; The Gallup Organization.

schools' performance—essentially, to fill out a report card on their schools by giving grades of A, B, C, D, and F. Just 16 percent of the respondents gave a grade of A to their schools. Most teens rated their schools as just good or average—a total of 37 percent gave their schools a B while 33 percent gave their schools a C. Overall, U.S. schools received a grade-point average, or GPA, of 2.27. In other words, U.S. schools earned a disappointing C average from their own students.

The teachers themselves received somewhat higher grades than the schools did. The Gallup Youth Survey asked the respondents to grade the first teacher they had that morning. A total of 34 percent gave their teachers an A, while 35 percent awarded them with a B, and 19 percent handed them a C. Overall, teachers earned a GPA of 2.86, or a C-plus.

Along with rating the teachers, students also rated extracurricular activities. A total of 34 percent gave an A to the sports, clubs, musical ensembles, and other activities available at their school, 33 percent gave the activities a B, and 20 percent gave them a C. Overall, extracurricular activities in U.S. schools rated a C-plus with a GPA of 2.82. Students also rated the technology available in U.S. schools. When asked about what they thought of the number and quality of computers in their schools, 28 percent of the students gave their schools an A, 33 percent gave them a B, and 20 percent gave them a C. Overall, technology scored a C-plus, with a GPA of 2.67.

With schools receiving these sub-par grades from the students themselves, is it any wonder that more and more of them are being homeschooled? However, educators have expressed many concerns about the homeschooling movement. They point out that school is a place where students learn more than just what is written on the blackboard.

In a school environment, young people are often called on to work in groups and solve problems as a team. In the cafeteria and the hallways, they learn how to interact with one another. On the athletic fields and concert halls, they learn leadership skills. These are all life lessons homeschoolers may not receive in their homes. "Home schoolers are often very astute," says Richard Shaw, dean of undergraduate admissions at Yale University in Connecticut. "But they often have to learn how to live with others."

Many homeschool advocates acknowledge that the home environment shapes students in a much different way than the school environment; however, homeschool students are proving through their standardized tests scores that the instruction they receive is more than adequate. A study conducted by the University of Maryland showed that the average homeschooled student scored in the 75th percentile on the Iowa Test of Basic Skills, an examination to assess progress in students' reading and math skills. On the Scholastic Aptitude Test (SAT)—the examination used by most American colleges to assess the verbal and math skills of applicants—the average score by homeschoolers in 2000 was 1100, about 80 points higher than the national average.

Parents who have taken issue with what teens read, consume, or learn in schools have accomplished significant change. Others have passed up their children's schools entirely to prove that the home can be a viable place to receive an education.

Glossary

ANTI-SEMITIC—Hating or discriminating against Jewish people.

ATHEISM—Disbelief in the existence of God.

CENSORSHIP—The suppression of certain books, songs, works of art, and other forms of creative expression that are deemed to have morally objectionable material.

CONTRACTION—The tightening of the uterine muscle shortly before childbirth, which occurs at more frequent intervals as the baby is pushed out of the womb.

DEPRESSION—An emotional condition characterized by feelings of sadness, hopelessness, and inadequacy.

HOLOCAUST—The mass slaughter of Jews and other European civilians by the German Nazis during World War II.

IMMUNIZATION—The administration of drugs to protect against disease.

LABOR—The process of giving birth to a baby, during which the child prepares to emerge and the mother endures considerable pain.

LICENTIOUS—Morally unrestrained, particularly in sexual conduct.

LITIGATE—To take a matter into court.

LOBBY—To attempt to persuade an elected official to support a particular cause.

PEDIATRICIAN—A physician who specializes in treating children.

PIOUS—Devoutly religious.

PSYCHIATRIST—A physician who specializes in treating mental illness.

PSYCHOLOGIST—A researcher, educator, or counselor who studies human behavior and provides remedies to behavioral problems.

REFERENDUM—The practice of submitting to popular vote a question posed by a government body.

Glossary

SOCIOLOGY—The science of studying relations among people.

TABLOID—Typically seen in large cities, a newspaper that specializes in reporting scandals and other sensational news.

VIZIER—In ancient times a high official of a Muslim state who usually acted as an adviser to the ruler.

Internet Resources

http://www.gallup.com

The Gallup Organization's web page features information on the Gallup Youth Surveys as well as the other polling work conducted by the organization.

http://www.nheri.org

Founded by homeschool advocate Dr. Brian D. Ray, the site for the National Home Education Research Institute presents statistics and research in support of homeschooling, as well as providing teaching resources.

http://www.fathers.com

The web page maintained by the National Center for Fathering provides reports, surveys, and polls about fathers and their jobs as parents. Young people can enter a Father's Day essay contest and nominate their dads for the "Fathering Hall of Fame."

http://www.divorcemag.com

Families in need of information on divorce can find answers to many of their questions on this home page of *Divorce* magazine. Articles about divorce and its impact on people's lives, answers to frequently asked questions, and even a humor column are available.

http://clinton3.nara.gov/WH/New/html/teenconf.html

The web site for the White House Conference on Teenagers includes transcripts, reports, press releases, and speeches covering topics that were raised during the event.

http://www.grandparenting.org

Dr. Arthur Kornhaber's Foundation for Grandparenting offers a number of resources for grandparents and grandchildren on its web page, including highlights of recent research by sociologists, reviews of books and videos, and bulletin boards where grandparents can find advice from other grandparents.

Internet Resources

http://www.parentstv.org

Composed of more than 800,000 members, the Parents Television Council keeps a close watch on what's on TV and what's not suitable for young viewers. The organization has rated dozens of TV shows and assigned ratings of "red," "yellow," and "green" to the programs. "Red" means the show is unsuitable for young viewers, "yellow" means parents should use caution, and "green" means the show can be viewed by anyone.

http://www.mediafamily.org

Founded in 1996, the Minneapolis, Minnesota–based National Institute on Media and the Family was created to help guide parents through the choices of entertainment and programming available to children. The organization's home page contains several studies on the impacts of violent and sexually explicit programming on children as well as tips for parents on how they can keep watch over their children's viewing and listening habits.

http://www.vh1.com/shows/series/movies_that_rock /warning/artists_speak.jhtml

This web page, maintained by the cable music channel VH1, has transcripts of testimony by Dee Snider, Frank Zappa, and other artists who appeared before the U.S. Senate in 1985 to argue against parental advisory labels. The site also includes musical clips from the "Filthy Fifteen"—the songs that were labeled offensive by the Parents' Music Resource Center.

Further Reading

Aydt, Rachel. *Why Me?: A Teen Guide to Divorce and Your Feelings.* New York: Rosen Publishing Group, 2000.

Cosby, Bill. *Fatherhood.* New York: Doubleday, 1986.

De Toledo, Sylvie, and Deborah Edler Brown. *Grandparents as Parents: A Survival Guide for Raising a Second Family.* New York: Guilford Press, 1995.

Gore, Tipper. *Raising PG Kids in an X-Rated Society.* New York: Bantam Books, 1988.

Kamlin, Ben. *Raising a Thoughtful Teenager.* New York: Dutton, 1996.

Pruett, Kyle D. *Fatherneed: Why Father Care Is as Essential as Mother Care for Your Child.* New York: The Free Press, 2000.

Ryan, Elizabeth A. *Straight Talk About Parents.* New York: Facts on File Books, 1989.

Wallerstein, Judith S., Julia M. Lewis, and Sandra Blakeslee. *The Unexpected Legacy of Divorce: A 25 Year Landmark Study.* New York: Hyperion, 2000.

Index

Numbers in **bold italic** refer to captions and graphs.

Index

Index

Index

Picture Credits

3:   PhotoDisc, Inc.
8:   Getty Images
10: R. Gates/Getty Images
12: © OTTN Publishing
14: Justin Sullivan/Getty Images
17: Corbis
20: Stockbyte
22: Lawrence Manning/Corbis
25: Bettmann/Corbis
27: PhotoDisc, Inc.
30: Stockbyte
32: PhotoDisc, Inc.
35: PhotoDisc, Inc.
41: Corbis
42: © OTTN Publishing
44: Stockbyte
48: PhotoDisc, Inc.

52: © OTTN Publishing
55: Stockbyte
58: PhotoDisc, Inc.
61: PhotoDisc, Inc.
64: PhotoDisc, Inc.
67: PhotoDisc, Inc.
70: Todd Buchanan/Getty Images
72: Alex Wong/Newsmakers/Getty Images
74–75: © OTTN Publishing
77: © OTTN Publishing
83: Bettmann/Corbis
86: Firefly Productions/Corbis
89: © OTTN Publishing
93: Corbis
94: Debbi Morello/Getty Images
99: © OTTN Publishing

Cover: (front) Stockbyte; (back) Stockbyte

Contributors

GEORGE GALLUP JR. is chairman of The George H. Gallup International Institute (sponsored by The Gallup International Research and Education Center, or GIREC) and is senior scientist and member of the GIREC council. Mr. Gallup serves as chairman of the board of the National Coalition for Children's Justice and as a trustee of the National Fatherhood Initiative. He serves on many other boards in the area of health, education and religion.

Mr. Gallup is recognized internationally for his research and study on youth, health, religion, and urban problems. He has written numerous books including *My Kids On Drugs?* with Art Linkletter (Standard, 1981), *The Great American Success Story* with Alec Gallup and William Proctor (Dow Jones-Irwin, 1986), *Growing Up Scared in America* with Wendy Plump (Morehouse, 1995), *Surveying the Religious Landscape: Trends in U.S. Beliefs* with D. Michael Lindsay (Morehouse, 1999), and *The Next American Spirituality* with Timothy Jones (Chariot Victor Publishing, 1999).

Mr. Gallup received his BA degree from the Princeton University Department of Religion in 1954, and holds seven honorary degrees. He has received many awards, including the Charles E. Wilson Award in 1994, the Judge Issacs Lifetime Achievement Award in 1996, and the Bethune-DuBois Institute Award in 2000. Mr. Gallup lives near Princeton, New Jersey, with his wife, Kingsley. They have three grown children.

THE GALLUP YOUTH SURVEY was founded in 1977 by Dr. George Gallup to provide ongoing information on the opinions, beliefs and activities of America's high school students and to help society meet its responsibility to youth. The topics examined by the Gallup Youth Survey have covered a wide range—from abortion to zoology. From its founding through the year 2001, the Gallup Youth Survey sent more than 1,200 weekly reports to the Associated Press, to be distributed to newspapers around the nation. Since January 2002, Gallup Youth Survey reports have been made available on a weekly basis through the Gallup Tuesday Briefing.

HAL MARCOVITZ is a Pennsylvania journalist. His other topics in the GALLUP YOUTH SURVEY series include sex, suicide, and race. He lives in Chalfont, Pennsylvania, with his wife, Gail, and daughters Ashley and Michelle.